# Praise for *Culture Spark*

Jason Richmond has knocked it out of the park. *Culture Spark* is the definitive guide to developing a winning culture. This is a proven groundbreaking system that every forward-thinking executive should read.

Marshall Goldsmith, *Thinkers50* #1 Executive Coach for 10 years and *New York Times* #1 bestselling author of *Triggers, Mojo*, and *What Got You Here Won't Get You There*

Every business culture needs an occasional tune-up. In *Culture Spark*, Jason Richmond provides business leaders with a proven 5-step blueprint for achieving this. He demonstrates how to reignite the startup mindset to develop an organizational culture that fuels long-term growth and inspires employee engagement and higher productivity. This book is truly worth the investment of your time!

Marsha King, PhD
President, SkillPoint Consulting

*Culture Spark* distills best practices for implementing culture change into a highly readable step-by-step program. Jason Richmond's years of experience ring through in this well researched guide that incorporates striking case histories from numerous organizations.

L. Balasubramanian
SIS Location Manager

If developing a culture that sustains long-term success is on your to-do list, *Culture Spark* is a must read. Jason Richmond maps out a 5-step plan that today's business leaders can take action on and execute with confidence and certainty.

Benjamin Collins
Founder and President, Connex Partners

Many authors define and discuss culture, but the common missing element is action. *Culture Spark* is a great resource for those who desire to go beyond theory and actually do something about their culture. Keep this book at your fingertips.

Sterling Gross, PCC
HR Senior Executive

Culture is not simply what we study and learn, it's what we are made of and able to share. Jason describes in the brightest, simplest, and most straightforward way a powerful framework for using company culture to create value. Definitely a strong weapon for any leader.

Leonardo De Biasi, Business Development Director
Techedge Group

# CULTURE SPARK

# CULTURE SPARK

## 5 Steps to IGNITE and SUSTAIN Organizational Growth

### JASON RICHMOND

IDEAL OUTCOMES

*Culture Spark: 5 Steps to Ignite and Sustain Organizational Growth*
by Jason Richmond

Published by

 IDEAL OUTCOMES

Chicago, Illinois
www.culturespark.io
contact@culturespark.io

ISBN: 978-1-7337105-0-3 (hard cover)
ISBN: 978-1-7337105-1-0 (soft cover)
ISBN: 978-1-7337105-2-7 (eBook)
ISBN: 978-1-7337105-3-4 (AudioBook)
LCCN: 2019934186

Edited by Melanie Mulhall, Dragonheart
DragonheartWritingandEditing.com
Book design by Nick Zelinger, NZ Graphics, NZGraphics.com

First Edition

Printed in the United States of America

# Contents

# Foreword

In a recent leadership forum, I sat in a room with several colleagues to tackle the elusive subject of organizational culture within an organization. If you're like me, I'm sure you have found it difficult to discuss such an abstract topic and have meaningful outcomes once the discussion has concluded. Sure, the brainstorms, retreats to the mountains, and workshops with costly consulting groups are great in the moment, but do we ever walk away from those experiences with a clear view that defines our organizational culture? And more importantly, do we leave these experiences with the ability to clearly articulate where an organization's culture will be tomorrow?

Organizational culture is the DNA of a company: How we get things done. How we treat customers. How we treat each other. With the ever-changing dynamics of the workforce, the stewardship of organizational culture is just as important as strategy, talent, product development, or customer service. It's so critical, that we spend countless meetings, team building events, and off-sites dedicated to the very subject. Like the secret ingredient to your family's most coveted recipe, the elements of an organization's cultural DNA are the strategic advantage that is impossible to replicate. The ingredients of culture, however, are not as easily crafted as a family recipe.

In *Culture Spark*, Jason Richmond provides a solution to this challenge with a practical guide for any leader responsible for shaping the culture of an organization. Through research and comprehensive interviews, Jason frames this guide with advice from executives, human resource professionals, and senior leaders from organizations across varied industries. Jason's guide serves as an excellent road map to help define your organization's culture today and plan how you may adapt it in the future. *Culture Spark* offers valuable strategies and practical solutions for clearly defining and shaping the culture of an organization.

As I'm sure you will agree, with *Culture Spark* in hand, you can ditch the retreats and meandering, feel-good discussions. *Culture Spark* will help you better understand your customer, your employees, and how you do business. Once you do, you will understand your culture. And until then, nothing else matters.

Andrew DeCaminada
Group Manager, Education, Training & Development,
Automobile Club of Southern California

# Introduction

*Leadership is absolutely about inspiring action, but it is*
*also about guarding against mis-action.*
–Simon Sinek, author of *Start with Why*

It happens to the best of businesses, and for numerous and varied reasons. After years of successful growth, sales level off. New orders diminish. Enthusiasm among the workforce wanes. Lethargy sets in. Creativity declines. Morale is low. Is it a time of crisis, or is this plateau simply a natural part of the business evolution, a time to pause and reflect, recharge batteries, and get ready for the next sales spurt?

A plateau isn't necessarily a bad place to be. If you're on a plateau, the assumption is you're at a rather solid vantage point. You have achieved financial and other goals and sit higher than many of your competitors. You've achieved success in getting there. At the same time, it's safe to say you have stalled in some way.

Perhaps revenues are not exactly stagnant but are simply growing at a much slower pace. Perhaps your organization is struggling with competition or the lack of innovation needed to enter new markets. Market share may be flat or declining. You may be losing some key talent. These are all likely signs that your business has the potential to falter and head in the wrong direction. Such challenges are common among startups, often with the magical number of $5 million being the milestone they need to climb past for ongoing success. But plateaus occur in all industries and in all sizes of companies, from startups to Fortune 100 organizations. Often, the common denominator is a problem with corporate culture. If that is the case, it's time to change your approach, reenergize your team, and both reassess and rethink your culture. Ignoring these signs could be deadly.

Why culture? Because the right culture makes or breaks an organization's success. It's as critical as business, operational, or financial strategy. Google "Why culture matters" and in a split second, you'll bring up more than a hundred million hits. Clearly, a lot of us are talking and writing about this subject. But if there is so much information and discussion, why do organization leaders and senior executives ignore the signs of culture erosion? And we can assume that they do because according to Dynamic Signal, an employee communication and engagement company, 51 percent of the US workforce is disengaged, causing massive losses in productivity—between $450 billion and $500 billion a year.

Perhaps we can take a lesson from startups. Lacking resources normally considered fundamental to success—such as deep pockets and large teams—some startups compensate with ingenuity, excitement, and energy. And they enjoy explosive growth.

Juggernauts like Facebook, Amazon, Apple, and Google continue to innovate and achieve stunning heights of success, while lesser companies find themselves stuck in a growth-inhibiting plateau. Buffeted by large egos, pushed into silos and turf battles, and drained by cumbersome rules and processes, these lesser companies stagnate. The passion and innovation dissipate, and the company flatlines. But exactly why? Let's first understand the challenges that cause stagnation.

## Problem One: Complacency

There's a silent killer that stalks many companies, and it's called complacency. These business entities may be riding high, celebrating success. Perhaps they've developed groundbreaking, revolutionary products. But they're resting on their laurels. They're market leaders, and they stop innovating because they don't think they need to. They don't look in the rearview mirror to see who and what is closing in on them and how the world around them is changing. Think Kodak, Hostess, Blockbuster, and Sears as examples.

Kodak invented digital photography but ignored this technology because it was wedded to its film-based business. Result: bankruptcy. Hostess, manufacturer of the iconic junk food Twinkie, failed to keep up with changing consumer tastes. Result: bankruptcy. Blockbuster, the nation's largest video rental chain (which itself was once a disruptive upstart), was steamrollered by Netflix. Result: bankruptcy. Sears, formerly America's top retailer, couldn't keep up with the low-price competition of Walmart and then the rise of Amazon. Result: Experts say the company is on the verge of bankruptcy. Go back further to Xerox or Montgomery Ward (which closed all its stores after 128 years, having been beaten down by Sears) to appreciate that this is not a recent phenomenon.

Xerox is a fascinating case. In 1959, the company launched the Xerox 914 photocopier, which revolutionized the document-copying industry, spitting out one hundred thousand copies per month—roughly 136 copies an hour or one copy every 26.4 seconds. There had never been anything like it before. It was such a stunning advance, it was even unveiled to the public on live television. Today, that performance seems quaintly slow.

Xerox established the Palo Alto Research Center (PARC), where its team of scientists and engineers developed transformational inventions including the mouse, the laser printer, and a windows/icon-based user interface. But Xerox management was content with its continuing profit from the 914 photocopier and didn't take advantage of their cutting-edge inventions. Instead, Apple, Microsoft, and Hewlett-Packard adapted the Xerox technology and made billions. Xerox, of course, is by no means a failure. But it could be a dominant force in today's computing world if it hadn't been complacent and settled for the status quo.

The message is resoundingly clear. Don't take your success for granted and orphan your latest offspring because you're so delighted with yourself for producing the ones you already have. Don't assume that the way you've always done things is working fine—an "if it works, don't fix it" approach. It is vital to get your people into the mindset that the future of the company depends on experimentation and never letting a big idea slip out of their hands.

Instead of a complacent culture, seek to foster a courageous culture. Encourage executives to go against the grain and push back when something doesn't feel right, even if it is wildly popular within your organization. Companies begin to fail when employees or leaders stop asking questions and become content.

## Problem Two: Disconnection to Values and Disconnected Values

Many organizations sculpt mission and corporate values statements. They hire copywriters to weave together flowery words that they feel will strike a chord with their customers and employees. Sadly, not too many of these companies make these values come alive. The words end up as posters on a wall or slogans on employee badges. While values are the foundation on which every successful culture is built, these companies fail to use them to guide decision-making, talent selection, or leadership development.

And even when organizations do make decisions based on corporate values, many fail to periodically evaluate those values. Sometimes values need to change, and the very process of examining the appropriateness of existing values can help drive a much-needed culture shift. This was the case when IBM made the strategic decision to transition from being a hardware company to being a technology service company. In 2003—long before social platforms like Facebook or Twitter became an indispensable part of everyone's lives—IBM executives held a worldwide values "jam," engaging its global workforce with the goal of refreshing company values. Over three days, tens of thousands of employees logged on to a company intranet site that let them participate in instant-message-style sessions about corporate values and how they shape employees' contributions. The participants posted, chatted, or shared their personal experiences about IBM values and how they had been lived out. It was the largest experiment IBM had ever done to engage employees globally, and it generated tremendous enthusiasm.

Aided by the sterling work of the IBM supercomputer, the jam discussions were analyzed over the following two months. How did employees envision IBM values and how did those values translate into behavior? The words *trust, invention, innovation,* and *client* were among those most used. Based on the results, the company updated its "basic beliefs" to resonate in the modern world. Customer service translated into "dedication to every client's success." Excellence meant "innovation that matters for the company and the world." And respect for the individual became "trust and personal responsibility in all relationships." These new values have served IBM for well over a decade and helped lay the foundation for a major culture and business strategy shift.

## Problem Three: Ego

Success creates egos, and egos breed power struggles. This is a major problem for many reasons, but mainly in the way egos can change the landscape of the corporate culture. Employees who credit themselves with a company's growth often see themselves as a cut above the rest. Egos quickly create an "us versus them" mentality, leaving little room for alternative thoughts and opinions. Ultimately, this causes a breakdown in trust, communication, and creativity, because other employees feel unappreciated or undervalued. Inevitably, dysfunction and contention permeate the entire company.

Leaders who have enjoyed long-term success often convince themselves that they have the Midas touch and become arrogant. They ask for input, but in reality, they just want to keep doing it their way. The best and brightest leave in frustration, seeking an environment where their voices are heard and where there is a greater sense of camaraderie.

## Problem Four: Misaligned Processes

As organizations grow and evolve, they often wisely create systems and processes aimed at establishing consistency and efficiency. There's no arguing that policies and protocols are necessary to keep a steady hand on the steering wheel of growth. But companies often fall into the trap of initiating a procedure to handle every step of the business or to solve every issue that might arise. Or they might conjure up policies that try to manage exceptions, or worse, bandage a problem rather than uncovering its root cause.

Even more insidious is when a company develops policies that are not aligned with core values—policies that might negatively impact its lifeblood of customers or demonstrate a lack of trust in its essential frontline employees. Think about the impact when every customer return must be approved by a manager. The customer has to wait, and the employee feels a definite lack of trust. Processes can quickly become a barrier to innovation. Sometimes less is more. There are many advantages to having fewer processes. Fewer processes usually translate to better ease of understanding and implementation for employees. Greater innovation is also enabled, and that makes for a more engaged workforce, which is vital for growth. When companies do not have a majority of the workforce engaged, they obviously are not getting into the hearts and minds of people to engender success.

## Problem Five: Micromanagement

When you survey employees, you often discover that micromanagement is a top complaint. It kills motivation, creativity, engagement, and job satisfaction. Employers need team members who will do more than what they are told, employees who will be creative and willingly try new approaches and solutions. Many of today's employees crave autonomy, so if you're running your business with a command and control, looking over their shoulder, second-guessing style, you will ramp up employee turnover. The first to go will be your top performers, as they'll find it easiest to snag positions at more open-minded, collaborative organizations.

As Andrea Belmont, Associate Project Director at Nielsen, told me, "Employees want to be given a chance to shine without a babysitter monitoring their every move. They want the freedom to prove themselves without their manager stepping in and correcting their actions before they've had time to figure it out for themselves."

Micromanagement not only cultivates a lack-of-trust culture and is one of the top three reasons people leave their jobs, but according to studies, it also elevates stress and causes other negative health effects. An Indiana University Kelley School of Business study of more than two thousand employees even found that those who had less control had a 15.4 percent increased chance of death.[1]

## Disengagement

These five issues—complacency, disconnection to values and disconnected values, ego, misaligned processes, and micromanagement—lead to the creation of the big one: a company culture teeming with disengaged employees. And this is an international predicament that needs to be resolved.

It is essential to discover why someone is disengaged to the point of quitting. Often, the cause can be traced back to their relationship with their manager. Consider that possibility, and ask questions like these: What did that employee experience? Was their manager an advocate for them? Were they encouraged to share their views? Was there opportunity for them to grow within the company and achieve promotions? Negative answers to these questions could well be the reason they're leaving.

When it comes to growing a small- to medium-sized business (SMB), the saying "Starting is easy, finishing is hard" has never rung truer. Automated marketing, crowdfunding, and other tools make it easier than ever to find customers and obtain enough financial backing to get a small business off the ground and continue to expand. However, I've found that organizations that have achieved exceptional success—reaching revenues between $100 million and $500 million—often hit a brick wall. Getting to the next level is more difficult than anticipated. Indeed, it takes something special to continue to knock through that wall. I'd argue that the "something special" is your culture. Here's why.

According to the Small Business Administration (SBA), small businesses (classified as those with less than five hundred employees) make up 99.7 percent of all US firms, which, in turn, accounts for more than 64 percent of net new jobs. Wow! Small businesses are adding new jobs faster than their larger competitors, but their share of total employment remains steady. While they are a huge engine of growth, most will never make it out of the small business category.

Why is it so hard for a small business to grow beyond the initial startup phase? Sometimes the market just isn't there for their product or service, but more often, it's a problem with their culture. Growth requires companies to successfully answer a variety of culture-related questions: Why do we exist? Who do we serve? How do we attract, hire, and retain the best people? What sets us apart from our competition? How do we empower people to grow the business year after year?

When you're in startup mode, these answers might be based on the founder's personal beliefs. But personality-based cultures often don't scale. Answers based on personal beliefs cannot become embedded in the organization and enable growth because people have very different personal beliefs. Answers must contain enough commonalities to become meaningful to every person. But how?

## Unlocking the Key to Culture

Culture is a shared, adopted belief system that allows employees to work together toward a common goal. It includes beliefs about mission and values, as well as beliefs about the work experience itself. The challenge is to articulate these ideas and beliefs in a way that is meaningful to employees.

This is more important than ever as younger generations enter the workforce wanting to work for purpose, not just a paycheck. They want to feel that their work is valued and that they are valued. They seek development opportunities. And unlike previous generations, these workers are not afraid to leave if those opportunities don't exist. These are key considerations for employers who want to attract and retain younger workers.

Beliefs are hard to change. Because of that, successful cultural change depends on discovering a common ground and reflecting on what people already believe. And that means involving and listening to your people.

When organizations prioritize culture, engagement improves. This drives tangible business outcomes, according to Gallup, that include a 24 percent decrease in employee turnover, a 10 percent boost in customer satisfaction, and increases of more than 20 percent in sales and profitability.[2]

Culture is the key to avoiding stagnation.

Involving your people in the creation of a shared, scalable culture is a must for businesses that want to continue to grow, regardless of an organization's size. Asking employees certain questions—like why they think the business exists, what its mission should be, and what values they believe should guide the business as it goes forward—is the first step to gaining buy-in and driving engagement. Creating an environment where individuals feel their input is valued and where they can grow along with the business is also key for growth.

Don't forget, though, that stagnation is not an automatic cause for panic, even if it is a time to seriously reevaluate who you are as a company. Slowdowns and plateaus are natural phenomena. But when you mention breaking out of a plateau, people are inclined to think that plateaus are downright bad and that you are in a rut. Plateaus are simply times to take a long, hard look at a company's position, appreciate how it got there, regroup, and plan where to go next.

Any organization, large or small, can avoid or recover from stagnation by taking a purposeful approach to building a culture that allows employees to thrive rather than simply survive. Let's get started.

# The Key Is the Culture

*I came to see, in my time at IBM, that culture isn't just one aspect of the game—it is the game. In the end, an organization is nothing more than the collective capacity of its people to create value.*
–Louis Gerstner, former CEO, IBM

When Richard Campo and business partner Keith Oden launched their real estate investment trust, Camden Property Trust, they knew one thing above all else: Their corporate culture was going to be nothing like the one they'd left behind.

It was the 1980s. Both men worked for an aggressive, fast-growth office developer in Houston, Texas. "It had a swashbuckling, pirate ship culture," Campo said. "The people at the top let people do whatever they wanted to do. They created silos that led to situations where people didn't collaborate and hated each other. To enhance your position, you used your prowess to make other people in other silos look bad. You became a street fighter. No one worked together as a team."

Then came the oil bust, and everything really fell apart.

"The company plateaued and then collapsed. If they'd had the right culture, they could have done very well. But the really smart people ran for the exits and created incredible organizations of their own."

Campo and Oden did a leveraged buyout of their group and around 1985, they started what became Camden Property Trust, a company that is today publicly-traded, with over $6 billion in assets and interests in more than fifty-five thousand apartment units. It's also ranked twenty-fourth on the *Fortune Magazine* 100 Best Companies to Work For list.

From the beginning, Campo said, they decided to build Camden in a totally different way from their prior experience and develop a positive, uplifting culture. "We wanted to be more collegial. We wanted to be more supportive. We wanted to make sure that as our organization grew, we didn't silo it."

The company started with two hundred people, but as it got bigger and broader, typical institutional issues arose. Staying collegial became more difficult. How did they tackle it?

"We had to put clear cultural statements in place. This is what we care about. These are our values. Here are our objectives. We built camaraderie through that. We were very specific in developing the culture we have today."

Campo and Oden were extremely conscious that success can lead to complacency and a business plateau, and they considered what they could do to prevent that. They brainstormed outlandish, hard-to-achieve goals. Camden's ambition? To prove the company was living up to its values by getting on the *Fortune Magazine* 100 Best Companies to Work For list. At their second attempt, they succeeded. In fact, the company went on to appear in the top ten for six years. In 2017, they were still on the list—but at number twenty-four, much to the chagrin of the employees. They asked themselves what they had done wrong.

In reality, only about fifteen companies have held a top ten position that long. "It's a rarefied area. It's hard to stay there," said Campo. Having the culture for employees to aspire to be on the list is "almost a self-fulfilling prophecy—part of their DNA."

Camden strives to instill the same values in its communities across the country following its established purpose: to improve the lives of its customers, employees, and shareholders one experience at a time.

When Camden first got into the *Fortune* top ten, it was around the end of the 2008 financial crisis. Predictions for the entire real estate industry were dire. Camden's stock price had dropped. They fought hard to avoid lay-offs, letting go of fifty-four people out of a workforce of 1,800. They froze salaries and cut bonuses. "We did all the things corporations have to do during a downturn. But the reason we went up the list was because we communicated with our people. We were out in front of it. We told them what we were going to do, and they appreciated that."

They lived up to their stated values, unlike other companies that blow up in a second when there's a disconnect between what they say and what they do.

"I think the foundational issues of culture get down to real simple concepts: trust, respect, credibility, camaraderie, integrity," said Campo, summing it up.

## What Is Corporate Culture?

While there are many ways to define what corporate culture is, Richard Campo's story about Camden Property Trust's corporate culture does a good job of exemplifying not only what corporate culture is, but why it is important. And culture is not just important, it's one key to getting off the plateau.

Here's my take on corporate culture. Culture encompasses how we share information and communicate with one another, how we treat people, how we make decisions, the kinds of policies (or lack of policies) we have, and how we are structured. Culture changes and evolves. In fact, it *needs* to change and evolve. Culture is not set in stone, and it's not one-size-fits-all. Culture must be aligned in a purposeful manner with your organization's business, operational, and financial strategies. Misalignment often causes organizations to plateau as employees lose trust or enthusiasm and can quickly derail even the best business strategy because it represents immediate and lasting barriers to execution.

Of course, new leaders often implement change as they apply their personal stamp on an organization, sometimes for the better, sometimes for the worse. To avoid destructive clashes with the existing workforce, it's essential to involve them and get them to embrace the new culture.

Some researchers have found that culture is more company-centered than industry-centered. Thomas Kell and Gregory T. Carrott, in a *Harvard Business Review* article "Culture Matters Most," reported that employees who work for the same corporation, no matter what their jobs, are 30 percent more likely to exhibit similar leadership competencies than people who do the same job but work in different companies.[3] This holds true even if the people from different companies work in the same industry or region. In other words, culture creates patterns and drives behaviors as much as behaviors and patterns create a given culture.

Let's examine some key myths and misconceptions that get in the way of the effort to formulate a desirable culture. When we appreciate the challenges, we can address the solutions.

## Myth #1. It's HR's Job

It's often assumed that because it's a "people thing," establishing or fixing corporate culture is the responsibility of the human resources department. Not so. While HR certainly plays a significant role in the *development* and *management* of policies that can help or hurt culture, it's the responsibility of everyone inside the organization to *create* and *maintain* a thriving culture. It's not down to one individual or one department.

The infusion of culture has to be embraced through all levels, from the top down, because it's a business problem, not a people problem.

In particular, it's imperative that the CEO and managers exhibit the culture's values because the workforce follows the everyday actions of its leaders. "If those actions are toxic, you're going to have a toxic culture. If they're engaging, you will have an engaging culture," says Stephen Hart, Vice President of Human Resources for the Federal Reserve Bank of Philadelphia.

## Myth #2. Perks Create Great Cultures

Who doesn't love great perks at work? Everyone appreciates a free gym membership or generous mental health days, but perks alone don't equate to culture. Perks are desirable. They can be fun and surprising. But culture is much more than a perk. Culture is about the emotional connection we have with our workplace—how we *feel* about working there. The right culture makes it easy for employees to create the connections needed to foster collaboration and unite teams as they work toward common goals. When we have common goals, we create cohesion. Conflicts become ways to improve things rather than ways to blame or finger-point. Cohesion also reduces duplication of effort and worse, the hurdles that result from people working at odds with each other. The right culture also reflects the opportunities employees feel they have been given to grow within a company and make valuable contributions to its success. When employees feel what they do matters, they are much more motivated to make the extra effort needed when times are tough or innovative problem solving is called for.

It boils down to how people are treated. You develop a first-class organization by winning hearts and minds. People rally behind their leaders when they feel their leaders believe in them, not because they've been manipulated with freebies and bonuses of one kind or another.

## Myth #3. Hiring for Culture Doesn't Matter

Hiring for culture does matter. Hiring people who don't believe in your values doesn't make sense because they are harder to acclimate with the processes and people you already have in place.

When you're recruiting, make sure your new hires are a fit for your culture. "If you just hire the smartest or the brightest, it may not work," says Chris Baggaley, Senior Vice President of Sales for the Auto Club of Southern California.

Keeping your culture at the forefront is even more important when you merge with or acquire another company. Charles Lilly, Program Manager, Talent Acquisition for Hub International, a network of more than four hundred insurances brokerages, knows that all too well. As a one-of-a-kind aggregator of insurance entrepreneurs with close to eleven thousand employees, Hub is constantly integrating new companies. Because of that, "We look at organizations that could be a good fit so it won't be a huge culture shock to them," Lilly says.

One thing you can't do is import another company's culture in the belief that you can make it your own. "It's tempting to think that because a company is known for its great culture you can simply hire one of its senior executives to bring that secret sauce with them. At some point, your culture has to organically manifest itself," says senior HR professional and executive coach Kerrian Fournier.

## Myth #4. Great Culture Is Expensive

Yes, it does cost money to give people a compensation and benefits package that makes them feel wanted and appreciated, but creating a truly great culture isn't dependent on lavish spending. Far from it. Providing low-cost elements such as the opportunity to be entrepreneurial and involved in decision-making, along with a focus on giving back to the community, are as important to employees today as health benefits or a 401(k). In the end, a healthy organizational culture enables your company to make more money, not spend it.

If you redefine the new workplace to embrace and celebrate individuality and empower people to achieve their full potential, you will be rewarded many times over—without having to invest a dime.

## Myth #5. Culture Is a Passing Fad

For many years, CEOs have shrugged off suggestions to work on their corporate culture. The realization that culture is not a buzzword but a vital long-term corporate attribute is finally starting to stick. And it is an historic shift.

Boards see the negative impact of a culture crisis on the value of their companies. Consider the recent sexual harassment crises at Uber and The Weinstein Company. These are just two instances of enterprises failing to take appropriate action. Uber's pre-crisis value of over $60 billion plummeted to $48 billion. A planned fire sale of The Weinstein Company collapsed when investors deemed the business's debt to be higher than it had been led to believe.[4] Lawsuits, investigations, and financial woes abound. As boards across industries assess the staggering costs when you ignore failing cultures, they will lay accountability at the feet of the C-Suite, and the CEO in particular.

Louis Gerstner's observation that corporate culture is *the* game tells you how vital it has become for farsighted company executives to understand and value the right kind of culture.

## Myth #6. Culture Is Created on Its Own

There is some truth to the statement that culture is created on its own. You already have a culture, even if you haven't consciously developed it. Culture is also what happens when no one pays attention, and then you pay the price.

Left to its own devices, culture often bubbles up negatively, hurting the growth and success of the company. As David Katz, Chief Marketing Officer for Randa Accessories says, "Culture is one of a company's biggest assets—until it isn't. Then it's one of its biggest obstacles."

Leadership and direction from the top are essential, but just as important is the need for leaders to collaborate with the workforce to create the right culture. No successful corporate culture has been built only from the top down. A grassroots build is just as important.

The bottom line is that you have to take responsibility to create the culture you want and not let your culture develop and evolve by chance. Your role is to ensure that your culture has been planned for and developed purposefully and intentionally. Leaving things to chance or hoping a newly introduced leader might solve all your problems is a quick path to failure or disappointment.

There are many definitions of corporate culture. The simplest: the way we do things around here. Florence Zheng, Global Head of Human Resources for software development company Bentley Systems says, "Culture is a solid foundation of shared beliefs and core values where there is a clear sense of purpose."

How do you know if your corporate culture is strong? "You know you are with a company that has a strong and healthy culture when you go to work, and it feels like camp," says Jana Greenberg, Director of Talent Acquisition for Horizon Media.

Who wouldn't want that? A great corporate culture is more than a place to work that feels like camp. It is also key to avoiding stagnation, loss of momentum, and achieving success. But what if your company was a great place to work?

# The Impact of Culture

*The right culture is about winning both the hearts and minds of*
*employees but without manipulation. No smoke and mirrors.*
*You have to be both genuine and inclusive.*
–Stephen Hart, Vice President Human Resources,
Federal Reserve Bank of Philadelphia

Culture is mission critical. If your company's culture is the embodiment of everything people do and believe, then culture clearly drives behaviors and decision-making. Winston Churchill once said, "However beautiful the strategy, you should occasionally look at the results."

Of course, strategy is important, and a differentiated strategy is even more important, but what is most important? Execution, which is how you implement the strategy so that it permeates your organization. And execution ties back to behaviors, which include what you say and do, consistently, day after day. You cannot risk a culture that's misaligned because that will always be a barrier to strategic execution.

Suppose one of your goals is to increase product speed to market, an achievement that's essential to your organization's ability to compete. If you don't have a culture that fosters cross-functional collaboration and trust, you won't be successful at executing the strategy to get there, no matter how important it is. The right culture is the foundation for effective execution.

But what is the right culture? And why does it matter? Is a healthy culture just a nice thing to have, or does it lead to meaningful financial returns? Numerous studies have shown that a culture that is good for the worker and the customer is also good for the bottom line.

One study in *The Journal of Organizational Behavior* posed a fundamental question: Which comes first, organizational culture or performance? Conducted over a six-year period and involving ninety-five automobile dealerships, the researchers concluded that culture definitely comes first. Companies that got good grades from employees on culture early in the study found that it led to greater customer satisfaction and higher profits. The ultimate conclusion was that there was a causal relationship between culture and performance, and it was culture that drove performance.[5]

A ten-year study by Queen's Centre for Business Venturing provided some hard statistics: Organizations with an engaged culture had a 65 percent greater share price increase, 26 percent less turnover, 100 percent more unsolicited employment applications, 20 percent less absenteeism, 15 percent greater employee productivity, and 30 percent greater customer satisfaction levels.[6]

Another well-documented study carried out by Harvard Business School professors Dr. James Heskett and Dr. John Kotter investigated how the corporate cultures of two hundred companies affected their long-term economic performance. The report, published in *Corporate Culture and Performance*, found that "strong corporate cultures that facilitate adaptation to a changing world are associated with strong financial results." By "strong corporate cultures" they meant cultures that highly value employees and customers and in which workers at all levels are encouraged to act as leaders. Over an eleven-year period, the researchers noted average increases for twelve firms with performance-enhancing cultures:

- Revenue growth: 682 percent
- Employment growth: 282 percent
- Stock price growth: 901 percent
- Net income growth: 756 percent.[7]

These are staggering results by any standards.

One major global study that set out to unearth the ideal employee work experience was a joint undertaking of The IBM Smarter Workforce Institute and Globoforce's WorkHuman Research Institute. They developed a new Employee Experience Index around key parameters: a sense of belonging, purpose, achievement, happiness, and vigor. They found that the highest scores on the Employee Experience Index translated into 23 percent higher performance, 40 percent greater discretionary effort, and employees who were 23 percent more likely to stay with the company.[8]

The stronger the culture, the higher the employee engagement. Teams with strong positive cultures can weather short-term blows to engagement, such as economic downturns, anxiety over mergers, or increased competition. In other words, culture is the fuel that drives and sustains positive engagement.

There's a huge risk in undervaluing the advantage the right culture provides. HR professional and executive coach Kerrian Fournier has been on both sides of the culture coin long enough to know that poor behavior and missteps in culture can be just as detrimental as missteps in foundational strategies. It still surprises her that so few CEOs actually consider their culture to be a critical business advantage.

But what is the "right" kind of culture? Is it as elusive as some executives might have you believe? If there is one common denominator, it is embodied in the word authenticity.

## Authenticity Matters Most

First and foremost, employees and customers alike crave the real deal. In an increasingly skeptical business world with shady dealings and data breaches increasingly commonplace, authenticity and honesty are traits high in demand.

But there's a growing authenticity gap. In a 2017 study titled "Authenticity in an Uncertain World" by global advertising, marketing, and communications company Fleishman Hillard, one of the findings was that nearly 84 percent of Americans equate a CEO's integrity with that of the companies they lead. And this was no small study. It involved nearly 5,500 consumers and almost three hundred companies in five countries. In essence, if a corporate leader is bad, the whole brand is viewed as bad. The study also showed that consumers take more than the quality of a company's products into account. Nearly half of their perceptions and beliefs about a company are based on the behavior of executives and the company's impact on society.

"Companies must embrace this new reality, operate in transparent and authentic ways, and align all aspects of their business with what the customer expects. Those that do will create a strong foundation of true value. Those that don't may not be around long enough to tell their story at all," says Marjorie Benzkofer, Global Managing Director of Reputation Management for Fleishman Hillard. The point here is that, more and more, the companies people elect to do business with are increasingly also the companies that people want to go to work for—in large part because they are a reflection of their personal values.[9]

An earlier study by global communications and public relations firm Cohn & Wolfe reached much the same conclusions. They asked twelve thousand people in the US and eleven other major markets to rate the top twenty desirable behaviors in a brand. Number one was "communicating honestly about product and services," followed by "not letting customers down" and "acting with integrity at all times." In other words: authenticity. Sadly, the Cohn & Wolfe survey reveals that only 3 percent of Americans believe that big businesses are honest and transparent.[10]

Recent exposés of outrageous data breaches at major social media companies, financial institutions, and huge corporations have only intensified the concern. Says Geoff Beattie, Global Practice Leader of Corporate Affairs at Cohn & Wolfe, "We believe this is the moment for big brands to take the idea of authenticity seriously. Our data tells us people around the world understand and value the concept."

The Cohn & Wolfe survey also asked consumers to provide their own definition of an authentic brand in a pithy 140-character tweet. The responses were consistent. Among them were these:

- An authentic company has values and morals and stands by them no matter what challenges are encountered.
- True to its missions and values.
- Does what it says, says what it does.[11]

What about the workers? In a survey of over 19,000 employees, conducted by *Harvard Business Review*, Georgetown University, and The Energy Project, only 46 percent felt they were respected by their leaders. Of those who felt respected, a whopping 89 percent expressed greater enjoyment and job satisfaction, and 56 percent said they experienced better health and well-being. Look where respect gets you.[12]

Interestingly, to get that respect from *employees*, the company must demonstrate the same characteristics identified by *customers* in the Cohn & Wolfe survey. "I've seen companies claim to be all about family or committed to sustainability and the customer, but when you observe their actions over time, you notice patterns that aren't aligned to those values—and it hurts their image. Whatever you are, be authentic about it to your employees and customers," says Craig Gentry, a former executive with Unilever Food Solutions.

Being authentic also means allowing individuals to display their individuality. Andrea Belmont of Nielsen is enthusiastic about her company's willingness to embrace all kinds of personalities. "I feel I can be myself here. I'm a huge nerd. I love *Star Wars*. I play video games. And the culture here is fine with that. As a result, I'm not afraid to share my interests with my colleagues. I'm not afraid to be who I am." While other companies have more formal, structured environments where expressing your personality is discouraged, Belmont finds Nielsen to be a place where employees can bring their personalities to work. And when employees can do that, they are being encouraged to be authentic.

The culture that fully embraces authenticity does so within (for the employees) and without (for customers). An Oracle report, "Four Ways to Build a Talent Magnet Organization," sums it up like this: "People gravitate towards authenticity—to the places and people who are what they say they are. Employees desire a workplace where talk is backed up by action; where there is no disparity between what a company does for its customers and how it treats its employees; where it embodies what it provides to the marketplace."

The report laments that in many organizations, there's a significant gap between the words and intentions of leaders and what employees experience. What are the obstacles? The report says, "Politics, ego, market pressures, internal competition, protecting one's turf—these can all get in the way of an organization being authentic and living its values."[13]

Companies need to take a long, hard, and honest look to see if they have a gap between what leaders say and what they do. If there is a gap, why does it exist? What can be done to narrow or eliminate it? Often, it goes back to having a mission and values and living by them, consistently, over time. Employees need to see that their leaders truly mean what they say. Chris Augustine, Senior Director of Technology, Global Advertising Intelligence at Nielsen says, "People need to know that the company, CEO and managers are willing to lead by example to follow the principles or pillars of culture that they have established. If the leadership team loses trust, it's often because they have contradicted what the company says their core values are comprised of."

Authenticity matters most.

## Approachability

Another key driver of trust that also starts at the top is approachability. Corporate leaders that operate with an ivory tower mentality are likely to find their tower tumbling down. Senior executives should be accessible and responsive, as opposed to keeping the C-Suite drawbridge up.

Among other things, approachability means not only having an open-door policy, but also demonstrating that it is more than lip service. "This strategy allows employees to feel secure knowing that their voices will be heard, their opinions will be respected, and their efforts will be appreciated," says Dan Calista, Founder and CEO of Vynamic, a healthcare industry management consulting company. Having a culture that embraces stepping forward and offering ideas enhances prospects of success, but it requires an understanding that not all ideas will be successful when implemented. "We're not afraid to 'fail forward,'" says Calista. "We've created a forgiving environment for taking chances, and sometimes it works, sometimes it fails."

This approach requires a fair bit of level-headedness and perspective when things do not go as planned or hoped for. It also requires a commitment to standing by your staff, as opposed to scapegoating anyone. Paul Stout, IT director for a privately held global firm, puts it this way. "In IT, mistakes can be expensive. But we do not point fingers; we do not blame. This allows employees to be open because it is nonthreatening. We work at keeping people's spirits up."

For Nielsen's Andrea Belmont an open-door policy is essential, but should be 360-degrees: "I want my employees to feel free to open up to me about any issues. I also want to be able to point out any missteps they have made, but in a positive not negative way." Getting feedback is important. Acting on it is essential. It is part of a continuous improvement mindset.

There's also a pragmatic reason for adopting a policy of openness. Chances are, if you're not transparent, whatever you're trying to hide will only leak out anyway.

## Culture and Engagement

Let's look briefly at the relationship between culture, engagement, and performance. First, it's important to clarify that culture and engagement, although tied to each other, are not the same thing. Engagement is how employees feel about the company and work environment. Culture is what they believe and how they behave. Beliefs are hard to change. So are behaviors. Feelings change more quickly. This is why a culture shift can take years, while improvements in engagement, with concerted effort, can occur in a few months or a few quarters. Engagement improves when employees feel respected, when they have the tools to do their jobs, when their opinions matter, when their bosses care about them as people, and when they feel they have growth opportunities. Engagement suffers in an unhealthy culture or when leadership does not follow through on its commitments. Disengaged employees can quickly sabotage a healthy culture.

## The Trader Joe's Difference

Trader Joe's is a prime example of how the right culture drives success when it is truly aligned with business strategy. The grocery chain has deftly balanced a combination of innovative products with a service-oriented culture to create a loyal customer base that continues to grow.

The stated mission of Trader Joe's is to offer value and a dedication to quality products and service through warm, friendly, committed employees. Employees—they call them crew members—are partly selected because of their enthusiasm and energy. Then they're thoroughly trained in product knowledge and communication skills and cross-trained in various store departments.

Addressing crew members at the opening of new stores, former CEO John Shields bluntly told newcomers that if they weren't having fun at the end of thirty days, they should resign. The company has seven core values: integrity, be product-driven, wow the customer, have no bureaucracy, be a national chain of neighborhood stores, Kaizen, and store as brand.[14] These values are embraced by the employees, which has helped Trader Joe's create powerful customer loyalty and stellar financial performance. In fact, on Glassdoor, employee ratings are 4.1 out of 5.0, with 85 percent of raters saying they would recommend the company to a friend, and 87 percent approving of the CEO.[15]

Trader Joe's has long focused on culture. A Graziado Business Report in 2007 described its merchandising approach as attempting to make grocery shopping "an exotic experience rather than an obligatory visit to market for staples." Their goal: to deliver an innovative and interesting shopping experience while offering hard-to-find, great-tasting products from around the world.[16]

What's the takeaway for you? It's your identity and not your product that is your foremost competitive advantage. It will always be much more of a struggle for your competition to copy who you are rather than what you do.

## The Right Culture Makes All the Difference in the World

It's not every day you walk into a company and immediately sense a culture rich with excitement, energy, and effectiveness. Tailored Brands, the retail holding company for men's apparel stores such as the Men's Wearhouse and Joseph A. Bank, is such a company. It is a company with over $3 billion in annual revenue and more than 30,000 employees,

Hector Pena, Senior Director of Strategic Sourcing and Procurement, told me that the pillars of their culture—customer service, belief in the people, communication, leadership, and respect—have been helping the company enjoy success, especially during the challenge of recent acquisitions.

Tailored Brands calls these cultural pillars **LION**:

Lead with the Customer.

Inspire the Change.

Own It Together.

Nurture the Community.

### Lead with the Customer

Pena says that the customer has to come first. "Without our customers, we have nothing. Without happy customers, we don't have sales." Customer service is often a make-or-break situation for any company, especially when a misstep can be instantly exposed on social media to hundreds of millions of people. At Tailored Brands, every conversation starts with the question "What does the customer want?"

### Inspire the Change

Inspire your team by trusting and not micromanaging. Build a culture that inspires high achievers. That means showing them you have faith in their abilities and ideas. Empower them to think outside the box.

Encourage curiosity, innovation, and smart risk-taking—all of which generate growth.

### Own It Together

How everyone works together makes all the difference in the world when you are creating and sustaining a meaningful culture. How you communicate, how you lead, and how you respect each other are all critical to that.

When it comes to communication, it's not just how you communicate, but what you communicate. Pena suggests that transparency "builds strong relationships that allow everyone to work together cohesively." Where projects are concerned, it is vital for team members to understand the entire scope of a project. In negotiations, even though management drives the process, final decisions are made by the whole team. And since everyone has been involved, implementation is easier.

How you lead is important, and leading by example is an essential element of that. Don't tell a story that you're not going to stand behind, says Pena. The CEO, leadership team, and direct managers must all lead through example if they expect employees to show long-term commitment to the values and goals of the company, and especially if the company needs to move beyond the plateau.

Respecting your employees gains their respect for you and leads to an overall improvement in the work environment and well-being of employees. "Many times, it's simply in the way we interact with our coworkers that improves the culture around us. It's the small things that make big impacts."

### Nurture the Community

Giving back is a significant part of the Tailored Brands culture. "Tailored Brands' employees understand that we do well by doing good," says Pena. "Whether it be raising awareness for breast cancer, helping veterans transition back into the workplace, or helping our own employees in need, we're all energized and our corporate culture strengthened when we give back to our community."

As a Fortune 1000 company, Tailor Brands' success stands out during a time when many retailers are struggling. In fact, Zack's Investment Research, a leading investment firm focused on stock research, analysis, and recommendations, gave Tailored Brands a buy rating in 2018, mentioning, among other performance factors, a 287.5 percent profit over the previous fiscal year. It is just another example of how a strong, positive culture helps drive performance.

## Procter & Gamble Cleans Up

When the right culture is in place, adversity can be turned into triumph when leadership and employees are aligned. There's a great example involving Procter & Gamble and their Vizir brand of laundry detergent (the forerunner of Ariel and Tide). Some years ago, a combination of drought and an unseasonal monsoon decimated most of the Philippines' coconut crop, the source of more than 90 percent of the world's coconuts. The price of the coconut oil, a key Vizir ingredient, rapidly skyrocketed, totally erasing Vizir's profit margin.

Just before this calamity, P&G had organized multifunctional brand teams to boost its sagging European business. The Vizir team swung into crisis mode and held an emergency session to consider every aspect of brand operation, including alternative product formulas, ways to cut costs, and ideas for simplifying the packaging.

By the end of one working day, they identified ways to make savings that fully offset the increased cost of coconut oil. In a few weeks, Vizir's profit margin was restored. Additional savings of the same magnitude were also clearly identified for the following fiscal year. Result: Vizir expanded across Europe faster and cheaper. Profits more than doubled from the pre-catastrophe period. Today, the combined sales in more than 140 countries of Ariel Liquid and its US cousin, Tide Liquid, make it the number one detergent in the world. They really cleaned up![17]

The Vizir story, though dramatic, is anything but a one-time sensation. The multifunctional team approach is now an institutionalized key element in the management of P&G's world brands. Operating in parallel to normal business units and functional groups, these brand teams streamline company organizational structures, supply systems, manufacturing facilities, marketing approaches, and distribution channels to such an extent that in fifteen years, the number of P&G billion-dollar brands grew from ten to twenty-two. For Procter & Gamble, a potential business disaster was turned into triumph through a culture of flexibility and dynamism.

## Creating a Positive Culture

But let's be clear. The challenge leaders face is that there is no one perfect culture. Culture needs to vary depending on your business strategy. The culture required to drive a strategy of innovation is different from the culture required to develop efficiency or operational excellence. There are many examples of healthy culture, and unfortunately, many more examples of unhealthy ones.

The *2018 DDI/The Conference Board Global Leadership Forecast* indicated six leadership megatrends. Culture was one of them. In their view, leadership strategies will fail without solid cultural cornerstones: clearly grasped and enlivened purpose, peer coaching, experimentation, psychological safety, and fully incorporated, diverse gender and generational views.[18]

I agree with these root requirements. Positive cultures need to have a focus on human relations, inclusion, commitment, and what I call organizational courage, or the willingness to go against the grain. Regardless of your business strategy, valuing individuals and appreciating their talents is critical.

"A commitment to employees coupled with a natural curiosity and openness to what they think are both key drivers of a positive culture," says Steve Gonzalez, Director, Major Projects Unit, Americas for KONE Corporation, a global leader in the elevators and escalators industry.

In my experience it's all about people, finding and keeping good people. And the only way to get good people is to actually treat them as if they're good people, as if they matter. One way of doing that is by creating a culture where everybody truly feels valued and respected.

When Diane Leeming headed up people strategy in Kraft's Cheese and Dairy business unit in 2011, she quickly recognized that its culture was multidimensional. She emphasized that leaders needed to hold people accountable, set goals, stop bad habits, and create business challenges.

One of the first ways to get started is by creating a culture where leaders hold one another accountable. She suggested actionable ways to inspire accountability:

- Start with hard numbers.
- Encourage freethinking.
- Communicate effectively.
- Address mistakes respectfully.
- Celebrate small wins.
- Avoid micromanaging.

Leeming also realized that setting high expectations was critical. "Small, easy wins are important, but for a massive company already decades into business, it was time to go big or go home." By setting high expectations, Kraft quickly found people aiming for success. "If you are intentional in what you expect from the business, you can turn things around."

The right culture lays the foundation for any organization's success, regardless of the industry, company size, or the phase of business growth. The right culture will allow you to attract better talent and retain such talent. Companies with a healthy culture gain a positive reputation, not only among employees, but also with customers and the market. Reputation drives your ability to attract new customers, retain those you have, and even to increase your prices. A positive culture will improve the quality of your employees' work, which further supports your reputation and brand image. If you do not keep pace with—or better yet, exceed—your competition in terms of your work culture, you are going to plateau or fall behind.

But what do you do if you do stagnate, plateau, or worse, your business actually takes a downturn? The answer is that there are strategies to reenergize you and move your organization forward.

# Getting from Here to There

*Plan for a culture that is exploratory—one that exploits your strengths.*
–Chris Augustine, Senior Director of Technology,
Global Advertising Intelligence, Nielsen

When entrepreneurs start a company, they focus on their product or service, how they are going to raise capital, and their target markets. They're passionate about their business and why they started it in the first place, a passion that typically attracts like-minded individuals. Usually, company founders drive the culture, based on their own beliefs about how a business should be run as well as what type of work environment will best serve the needs of the organization. There is clarity of purpose because that purpose resides in the minds and hearts of a select few.

Such passion is critical for many reasons. Revenues are often low, and cash flow might be a challenge to such an extent that the founder and other believers often forego some level of compensation for the good of the company. Typically, this core group is very hands-on, taking care of a wide range of functions, ranging from business development and marketing to operations, human resources, and accounting. As revenues grow, the organization adds employees with more specialized experience to handle these functions. The fast pace of growth is exciting and, for a period, keeps the team focused and aligned.

There comes a point, however, where the profusion of new additions starts to dilute the company's focus and purpose. In part, this is a natural result of segmenting the business into functional areas and hiring new leadership to oversee them. But that dilution is further compounded as the founders become less involved in the day-to-day operation of the company when their attention is rightly drawn to investor relations and growth strategy. At this stage, organizations often consider acquisitions to speed their growth rate. Although this can be a wise financial or market share decision, acquisitions quickly and powerfully further dilute the original culture. So it's important for leaders to keep in mind that the company they started will not be a startup forever. It's inevitable that the culture of the organization—the "how we do things around here"—will evolve.

Entrepreneurs often lose sight of the cultural implications. So certain that everyone still thinks like *they* do, they completely miss what is often a subtle yet impactful culture shift. This is because cultures do not shift overnight. It's similar to the way we slowly gain weight as we age or change our diet and exercise habits. One day we wake up and realize that we're fifteen pounds heavier. We ignore the slow, imperceptible change until we get on the scale or try to put on a pair of pants we haven't worn in a while and are shocked at the difference. Maintaining good health and fitness takes work. So does sustaining a healthy, fit business culture. Leaders need to ask a very important question, ask it often, and listen to the answers: Who do we want to be when we grow up?

Recognizing that the culture is no longer serving our needs and is a barrier to success is hard enough, but knowing where and how to start to change it can be even more daunting. The Culture Transformation Model below is not complicated, but it does provide a clear road map for business leaders to avoid culture dilution, regardless of their stage in the business development cycle.

## Culture Transformation Model

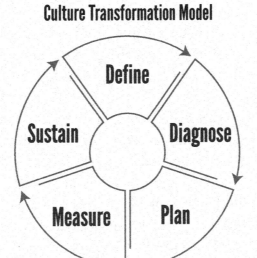

## Define

Before you can begin to change your organization's culture, you need to clearly determine and articulate it:

- What is your organization's purpose?
- What are the values you want every employee to align to?
- What core beliefs are critical to you from a business perspective as well as from a personal one?
- What kind of culture do you want for your organization?
- Will this culture align well with your business strategy?
- What risks or gaps might this culture create?
- Who do you want to be as you continue to grow?

My team and I have asked dozens of leaders across a wide range of industries "Who owns an organization's culture?" Their answers were nearly 100 percent consistent: It is both top down and bottom up, but the CEO and the C-Suite are responsible for purposefully and intentionally creating and communicating the vision and modeling it.

If you don't take charge and define the culture, it will define itself without your conscious involvement. And that's never a good thing. Andrew Koehler, Human Capital Management Consultant for ADP, says, "When it goes right, it becomes hard to sustain. When it goes wrong, it's hard to turn that ship around, whether you are fifty or five hundred people."

The best approach leaders can take is to make it deliberate and part of their overall business strategy. There has to be clarity at the top. The CFO, CHRO, and CEO need to be in sync on it. In fact, the entire C-Suite must be engaged and involved. And the impact of your changes must be constantly monitored and measured. It is true that you will fail if you don't know how you're doing, but it is equally true that you will fail if you don't know where you're going.

You must have an intentional, farsighted outlook. At Emerson Automation Solutions, Tony Norris, Vice President, Global Sales for Rosemount Flame and Gas products, advises, "Start with the long-term goal. Too many leaders start down the path of what they can do straightaway rather than looking long-term." He adds that this process needs to be led and fully owned by the leadership—and it is their actions that will be noted. "Leaders need to keep in mind that their actions, and not their words, are important. Employees watch you closely and will emulate your behavior. You are not going to drive culture change just by telling people what to do."

It's also important to remember that middle management is a key driver of culture. They are closer to the rank-and-file employee than senior executives and therefore have a very strong influence, especially when you have a remote workforce.

By exploring and defining your desired culture collaboratively, you gain support and buy in, both critical to success. Changing your culture is never easy, and you will need passionate support from all levels of your organization to make this happen.

# Diagnose

You wouldn't want your doctor to prescribe treatment before making a thorough diagnosis of your illness. Yet, companies and their leaders often try to "fix what's wrong" without first determining what is not working—or, conversely, and just as important, what is working. The most common challenge I see is that when you ask a lot of employees about their organization's culture, you get a lot of different answers, and most of them won't be very precise. Even more astounding is the lack of congruency when you ask this question of senior leaders.

Another important reason to thoroughly diagnose your company's culture is that it is just too easy to blame the culture when things go wrong. But when your strategy is not moving forward, it may be that the culture is trying to tell you something about your own leadership philosophy. In fact, it may not be the culture at all. It might be you. The key is to avoid blaming your culture. Instead, use it intentionally. And to do that, you must have a deep understanding of what your culture is, not what your perception of the culture is. A thorough diagnosis is critical for proper treatment.

You can start by talking with people. When David Starr, VP of the Commercial Real Estate Group for Northern Trust Corporation, joined the company, he had coffee meetings with thirty different executives in the first month. He went prepared to pepper them with questions about their personal experiences. "As a result, I knew who the people were, and I knew what they were trying to do. It was very much a hands-on effort to get acquainted with the culture."

Begin by asking your senior leaders some basic questions. Then put together focus groups and ask them questions regarding your current culture. When putting together such groups, think about their makeup. Your will want different perspectives, so make sure your various groups consist of varying levels of employees in different departments or business units. Bear in mind that some employees may not be as honest if there are managers in the room, so you might want to have frontline employees in their own sessions, separately from their managers, and managers separate from their directors or vice presidents. Also, bear in mind that employees may not be honest about culture if the existing culture is one in which people know that there is a company line with which they must agree or their jobs will be in jeopardy and/or if the culture is one in which the messenger is killed. In some organizations, focus groups need to be led by someone outside the organization who will maintain the anonymity of participants. The point is to get at what people really think, and the groups need to be structured in a way to make this possible. Suggested questions include the following:

- How would you describe the culture here? What key words or phrases come to mind immediately?

- Have you seen or experienced a change in our culture during your tenure? If so, describe it.

- Which changes have been beneficial? Which have been detrimental?

- What do you think has caused the culture changes you have seen?

Compare their answers. Note where you find agreement and where you find differing opinions. This approach gives you the foundation for further analysis and information gathering about the state of your current culture. Compare these answers to the data you have from other sources, such as employee engagement surveys, focus group notes, and exit interviews. These are all tools that deliver considerable insight into your culture as experienced by your leaders and employees alike.

Another way to diagnose your culture is to get out of your office. Spend time with all levels of employees, both formally and informally. Walk around. Management by walking around (MBWA) was popularized in the 1980s by Bill Hewlett and David Packard and later recommended by Tom Peters and Robert Waterman in their book *In Search of Excellence*. Today, many leaders have revitalized the concept, and with good reason. Getting out of your office brings you face-to-face with employees you would otherwise never encounter, employees who provide insights and observations that might easily be missed if you depend solely on reports from higher up the ladder.

The underlying reason for a thorough diagnosis is to help you and your team reach consensus on your current culture and subsequently on the desired future state.

## Plan

Once you've diagnosed your culture, compare your findings with that of the culture you desire from the perspective of both your leadership team and your employees. A gap analysis will help you determine next steps. One thing I know for sure from my clients and the many leaders I have interviewed is that changing or reviving your culture never happens by chance. Planning is critical because your intervention strategies must be intentional and purposeful.

As you plan, consider all aspects of your business. Connect your plan to your values and the desired culture you defined. Examine the behaviors of your leaders, middle managers, and employees in relation to those values. Where are there disconnects? "The everyday actions of leaders establish the culture," says Stephen Hart of the Federal Reserve Bank of Philadelphia. "If they are toxic, you are going to have a toxic culture."

Hart also says that you should take a serious look at your organizational design. Is it top-down? How many layers of management are there? Do your systems and support structure align with your desired culture and values or are they barriers?

Here are some other questions you need to ask: Is there a suitable rewards and recognition program in place? Are policies and procedures designed to control behavior, or do they enable people to make decisions and act? Are managers flexible or intolerant? Does human resources police and set a tone of distrust, or are they open to developing potential?

Above all, Hart says to ask this question: Is there a shared vision of the future that is communicated thoroughly throughout the organization?

A part of the planning process needs to involve honing your statement of what you want corporate culture to be so it is simple and understandable. "Somebody in the executive leadership team has to know and articulate the culture they want," says Jonathan Evans, Senior Vice President of Communications for ThyssenKrupp North America. "Then, for communications people like me, it becomes a matter of recruiting people who will become missionaries for the culture and make that vision reality. It's important to keep the culture message as simple as you can. The more complicated you make it, the tougher it is to explain and drive."

## Measure

Without measurement, there is no accountability. *Inspect what you expect* is an old saying that some people interpret as meaning that follow-up is necessary. While follow-up is certainly important, I believe the saying has a deeper meaning. If you do not measure progress and track it, you are going to be disappointed by what happens—or does not happen. Measuring your progress as you lead your culture transformation is a vital part of inspecting. And inspecting creates accountability. Inspect what is important, what people agreed to act on, and whether results are sustained.

What should you be measuring? Think about measurement from two perspectives: behavioral/qualitative outcomes and business outcomes. Both are important. To ensure alignment with your business strategy, begin with business outcomes. What are your key business goals, what is your baseline, and where do you want to be? Next, identify current gaps. Then identify key actions you need to take to close those gaps. Do the same with related behavioral/qualitative outcomes.

Many of the actions you identify and put in place will take time to produce results, so you can't wait until the key actions you delineated are completely executed to see if you are making progress. This means you need to identify a few *leading* indicators that will help you ascertain whether progress is being made. The template below, Culture Shift Strategy, illustrates these concepts. In this fictitious example, the business strategy is to shift from an operational excellence, process-driven culture to one that is more customer-centric.

One of the key measures our sample organization uses is Net Promoter Score and, as such, you will see it mentioned several times in the template. Net Promoter Score gauges the loyalty of a firm's customer relationships. It serves as an alternative to traditional customer satisfaction research and is correlated with revenue growth.

## Culture Shift Strategy

| Strategic Goal | Current State | Desired State | Planned Actions | Leading Indicator Measures |
|---|---|---|---|---|
| Shift from operational excellence to customer-centric core competency | **Business Outcomes** Customer satisfaction scores as measured by Net Promoter Score 6 | Net Promoter Score 9 | • Company-wide communication plan on new strategy and its ties to company values | **Business Outcomes** Monthly NPS surveys of customers |
| | 70% of our business is repeat business | 90% of our business is repeat business | • Customer service training | Monthly data on repeat business percent

Quarterly turnover of CSRs |
| | **Behavioral/Qualitative Outcomes** Customer Service Survey: 80% feel our policies are not customer-friendly | 10% | • Training for managers on how to coach customer-service skills | **Behavior/ Qualitative Outcomes** Pulse survey on reaction to communication |
| | Customer Service Rep (CSR) Survey Engagement Scores: 70% are engaged or highly engaged | 85% | • Revamping hiring process for CSRs • Review and rewrite top 15 customer policies | Quarterly CSR survey on policies, training, and management coaching |
| | 60% would take another job if they had the opportunity | 35% | • Customer focus groups | Quarterly evaluations by managers on service performance |
| | 40% feel they are adequately trained and coached on how to provide better service | 80% | | Quarterly engagement pulse surveys of CSRs |

# Sustain

Clearly, ongoing measurement enables you to adapt your plans quickly. If an intervention or plan is not working, you want to know sooner rather than later so you can make adjustments. In our example above, you don't want to wait six months to find out if customer service reps are getting value from their training. Similarly, you also want immediate feedback from key customers on their experiences with changes in company policy.

As I mentioned earlier, measurement creates accountability. You want to know if your managers are actually scheduling coaching and one-on-one sessions with customer service reps and whether the customer service reps feel these discussions are valuable.

Sustaining your culture requires more than measurement and follow-up. A key component is communication. Tony Norris learned some things when Emerson embarked on a strategic culture shift. His advice is to leverage all your resources. When you have a vision, bring others in to help execute it. Don't feel you have to provide a detailed execution plan because doing so only stifles their input. And don't just rely on internal resources. Use expert training consultants to bring in fresh perspectives.

Managing a culture shift can take on an energy of its own. The initial stages require intense attention, stimulating excitement, and an intimate awareness of actions.

But as time passes, the trend is for companies to decrease their attention and awareness of their goals. To combat this, it is vital to keep culture at the forefront of meetings, conversations, and everyday life. Leaders must lead by example and continue to demonstrate company values. Recognition and rewards need to be targeted at the changes you are trying to drive and implement. Furthermore, continued training is essential to keep employees engaged in the mission and help them understand the benefits that go with it.

And above all, balance a sense of urgency with patience. As Danielle Brown, Intel's Chief Diversity and Inclusion Officer, emphasizes, "Culture change takes time. It's messy. It's really hard. And you absolutely have to be committed to this for the long haul and be okay with some bumps and some learning along the way."

We're going to drill down on each of the components in the Culture Transformation Model—define, diagnose, plan, measure, and sustain. But sometimes it's helpful to take a look at an example of a desirable end result before we begin to drill down on components, just to remind us what is possible. The Cardinal Health experience demonstrates that the right culture gets results.

## Cardinal Health: Great Culture, Great Results

Every company wants and needs to make a profit. When the company can also deliver improved health for consumers along with inspiration and training for small entrepreneurs, so much the better.

Cardinal Health, a Fortune 500 global health care services and products company, does all of that. Its culture, which focuses on bettering lives, helps drive success. And it's obviously working. "You know you have a good culture when you have a company with more than fifty thousand employees and it feels like a small company," said Jason Watt, Director of Sales in Pharmaceutical Distribution.

But what does Watt and other members of management do to instill that small company culture in such a big, diverse corporation?

### *The Right People*

Watt says it's imperative to have the right people in the right positions.

The right people are knowledgeable and deliver improved customer service. That helps customers better understand Cardinal Health's message and direction. Cardinal is operating in a fast-changing industry. That ability is critical. "Over the last two years we have had some major shifts in the industry that affected both our customers and our business," Watt told me. "Having the right people helped us to better educate our customers, execute initiatives, and increase our customers' success."

### The Right Mindset

The right people in the right seats also need to have the right mindset—a positive one, especially during a time of uncertainty.

Many of Cardinal Health's customers were faced with lower profitability due to shifts in the industry. Some even had doubts whether their business could survive. Said Watt, "Having a team that remained levelheaded and upbeat had a positive impact. We helped our customers see new opportunities to cut costs, better consult patients, and find niches within different business models to drive success and keep their doors open."

### A Winning Culture

Watt focuses his team on setting milestones and goals, celebrating success, and looking at defeat as a way to learn and adapt to better execute the next time. This attitude has driven the acquisition of new customers and is helping them achieve their aspirations.

### A Family Team

When you have a team you enjoy working with, you have fun. And fun is a contagious thing. Combine that with everything else being aligned, and you become unstoppable. "Happiness drives happiness and makes the bumps in the road softer," said Watt. "Trust is established more easily. Learning happens faster. Work isn't work." When you love what you do, it fits into your life organically. A culture that supports this way of working infuses not only the entire organization but also that organization's customers.

### Truth and Transparency

Results of employee engagement surveys at Cardinal Health are shared and discussed openly at an all-team meeting. This group debates opportunities and brainstorms ways to improve scores. Small teams are then encouraged to continue the dialog, focusing on the top three issues that directly impact their team. Volunteers lead actions to hold the team accountable. For this to work well, team members must feel that it is safe to speak up and believe that they will be respected and supported even if what they say is not what their manager or other team members want to hear.

### The Right Kinds of Reward and Recognition

Watt encourages his team members to put themselves in their customers' shoes. Deeply understand their business and goals. Look for pain points and concentrate on alleviating those pains.

"We integrate that knowledge and behavior into the culture by rewarding that behavior both formally and informally," Watt said. "We recognize and praise our teammates when we see it." Cardinal Health's incentive plans are built to also drive that behavior, and teammates are score-carded on both what is accomplished and how it was accomplished.

The right kinds of rewards motivate and inspire people. "Set high expectations, measure them, and inspect what you expect. You want to avoid setting fires under people, but instead, build a fire within people."

### Getting Results

Watt shared that his team scores for engagement were typically among the highest in the organization. He attributes this to his focus on development and career planning. "Being a leader is being a good coach. This is driven from the C-Suite down. We grow talent from within."

Among other things, this means understanding their strengths and weaknesses, supporting their career goals, consciously connecting team members for mutual learning, and sharing best practices to encourage collaboration instead of competition. He also helps his team members understand what the customers' challenges are and how to help them adapt to change.

"Ultimately," he says, "you have to allow people to walk down their own path, but don't let them accidentally jump off the cliff."

———

Of course, this dynamic balance between leadership support and individual responsibility is optimally possible when an organization has clearly defined purpose and values. In fact, having a clearly defined purpose and values is critical to the creation of the corporate culture itself and equally critical for financial success.

# Defining Your Culture
# through Purpose and Values

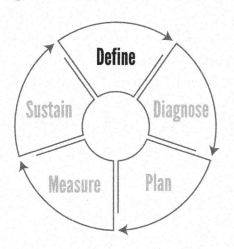

*Effectiveness without values is a tool without a purpose.*
–Edward de Bono, author and inventor

Defining the culture you want in a planned and intentional manner is critical both for your short-term and long-term success. It doesn't matter whether you are leading a startup or running a more mature organization whose culture is no longer healthy. After all, your culture is your identity. It reflects how you see yourself and how the outside world sees you.

The inherent need for a corporate culture is compelling. Put groups of people together to work and the culture will naturally emerge and evolve. But will it be one that serves your organization well? If you and your leadership team do not define the culture, model it, and nurture it, the vacuum will be filled, and you probably won't like what dust it gets filled with. Without a well-defined culture, you are leaving the number one guiding force for your organization up to chance.

Don't forget that culture is an emotional mindset. Do you believe in what your organization does? Do you like being there? Do you respect how your organization makes decisions and how it treats employees, customers, and other stakeholders? These are not business operations questions, they are emotional questions that require answers that satisfy those emotions.

So what are the components of a well-defined culture? Basically, they include your purpose, your values, your core business strategy, and your core people strategy. But it all starts with purpose and values.

## Purpose

Purpose is all about the "why" of being in business. Why does your organization exist? Purpose creates an emotional connection, and at its core, culture is an emotional mindset. Purpose is not about how you make money and it is not about creating shareholder value, although most executives are clearly of the mindset that companies with a solid, well-articulated purpose are more successful at making a profit.

Purpose is about the underlying reason for existing. Purpose addresses what problem you are trying to address and the value you are adding to customers and to the world. Purpose is a critical component of your business strategy. Without a clearly defined purpose, employees have no shared intent, and your organization will struggle to have a long-term perspective. Purpose also engages your customers. When you let your purpose drive your business strategy, you take a more unified, holistic approach to decision making and actions. Jason Watt of Cardinal Health states the purpose of Cardinal Health in a way that is not only succinct but also transcends the business objective of making money. "We are in business to better people's lives, to provide quality patient care, and to help pharmacy owners build their small-town, independent businesses."

People want purpose. They are not merely driven by business results—though business results are essential. Purpose is what inspires people to do more than put in their hours. Purpose creates a shared rallying cry for your employees.

Unilever's Domestos bottled bleach is a good example of this. There may not be a humbler, less sexy product than Domestos bleach. It's a brand that has been around since the 1920s, when traveling salesmen on bicycles sold it door-to-door throughout the United Kingdom, and it found the perfect home when it was acquired by Unilever in the 1960s. Unilever, founded in the late 1880s by William Hesketh Lever, helped popularize cleanliness and hygiene in Victorian England with a product called Sunlight Soap.[19] Today, it is waging war on germs and promoting hygiene where people are most affected: emerging markets. It is improving the health and lives of people and communities around the world. Through its social mission, Domestos, in partnership with UNICEF and social enterprise eKutir, it is on target to help twenty-five million people gain improved access to a clean toilet by 2020. The purpose certainly elevates the product and the morale of employees.

A simple, clearly articulated purpose inspires your team to do good work for you because it articulates the work you do *for someone else*. It needs to be a simple, declarative sentence that's a bold affirmation of a company's reason for being. Here are a few examples of major companies that have sculpted well-thought-out purpose statements:

- Nike: "To bring inspiration and innovation to every athlete in the world." Nike's cofounder Bill Bowerman said, "If you have a body, you are an athlete." Clearly, Nike's purpose is about more than athletic shoes and sports apparel.

- Starbucks: "To inspire and nurture the human spirit—one person, one cup and one neighborhood at a time." Inspiring and nurturing the human spirit is about more than coffee.

- Southwest Airlines: "To connect people to what's important in their lives through friendly, reliable, and low-cost air travel." Southwest knows that it is about more than getting from point A to point B.

- Uber: "Evolve the way the world moves." It's more than a car service and much more than a taxi service.

- Mary Kay Cosmetics: "To give unlimited opportunity to women." This is about women's lives, not just makeup.

### Lead a Purpose Discussion with Your Team

What is your corporate purpose? Keep the examples above in mind as you analyze your mission and its relevance in the world. How do you define what you do in a way that expresses your contribution to society? Begin with these questions:

- What do we do?
- Why do we do it?
- Why is it important to others?
- If we went away tomorrow, what would our customers lose?
- How do we make our customers feel?

As you gather input and have discussions, you will be able to fine-tune your wording. Assemble your favored purpose statements and then run through the criteria questions below.

## Purpose Statement Criteria and Evaluation

**Purpose Statement** _____

| Criteria | Evaluation: Yes/No |
|---|---|
| 1. Is it a contribution to society (not a product or service)? | |
| 2. Does it answer this question: Why is this work important? | |
| 3. Is it brief and memorable? | |
| 4. Does it use powerful words? | |
| 5. Does it unite efforts and inspire action? | |
| 6. Is it truly authentic to us? | |

It's important that leaders kick off this process. But leadership voices are not the only voices that need to be heard. Gain input from a diverse range of employees. There are several approaches to doing this. You and your team can decide what makes the most sense for your organization. Here are some options:

- Your direct reports conduct similar discussions with their teams.

- Your direct reports show the purpose statement to their departments or business units and ask for feedback.

- If you have an internal social media platform, you use it to gather feedback from a wide range of employees.

- You hold an employee contest to craft a winning purpose statement.

## Values

Values are the cornerstone of your culture. According to Wil Reynolds, founder and CEO of digital marketer Seer Interactive, "Values are the foundation, but only if you really live them and model them." He's right, but unfortunately, most organizations come up with a list of generic values, put them on a poster, and stop there. Values need to be customized to your organization and described in everyday, relatable language. I cannot emphasize enough that they need to serve as a guide to business decisions and a blueprint for all business actions.

Reynolds shared a story with me to illustrate one of Seer Interactive's core company values: transparency. It was so instilled in the attitude of employees that it displayed itself even when they were leaving for opportunities elsewhere. One team member not only gave four weeks' notice, which wasn't required, but also cared enough to submit the résumés of people she felt would be a good replacement. Another woman gave the company two-and-a-half-months' notice, confident she would not be terminated early because she understood and trusted the corporate culture. Leadership at Seer makes a point of telling employees that they won't be tossed out the door if they give notice.

Values need to be communicated and instilled into the culture from the company's inception. And they need to be lived, not just given lip service. If you do that, they will help sustain your culture during tough times and during periods of rapid growth.

Values are not the same as beliefs. It is easy for beliefs to change or to be changed when they are painful, costly, or simply inconvenient. Perhaps the sharpest example is the infamous downfall of Enron. CEO Jeffrey Skilling was tried on thirty-five counts of fraud, insider trading, and other related crimes. He maintained his innocence from the first day of his trial to the day of his sentencing. The evidence presented in court was to the contrary, but it was probably public opinion that was most damning.

Among the ammunition used by journalists and commentators

was a company-produced book, the *Enron Code of Ethics Manual*. The sixty-four-page manual not only outlined the company's mission and core values but also gave the policies on ethics that all employees were expected to follow. The core values Enron touted were communication, respect, integrity, and excellence. Enron talked a good game, but didn't honor any of them. The bottom line is that values are meaningless if they are not lived—which includes being used as a mirror in decision making. Enron and Skilling failed in every way, and today Skilling has plenty of time to reflect on the error of his ways while serving a sentence of twenty-four years and four months in federal prison.

A complete contrast to Enron is the ethical values established—and lived—by Emerson Automation Solutions. Emerson's Tony Norris says that his company has clear orders from the top down on how they want the company run. "For our company, abiding by our ethics is more important than dollars."

The criteria over what is acceptable and not acceptable in business have been evolving for years, but at Emerson, its ethics standards make it easy to do business the right way, every time. Not only is this important for the company's reputation, it is critical to employee and public health and safety. "Oil and gas companies are dealing with processes that can be very dangerous. We would never chase a dollar if it's going to put somebody in an unsafe environment. Our customers expect it and know they can count on us to follow through."

To ensure they are following industry best practice safety measures, Emerson holds regular practice-based training through scenarios to measure reactions and responses. This real-life form of training prepares their employees as no computer-based or classroom training could, and it is just part of the company's commitment to high ethical standards.

"Most of our clients are large corporations very much in the public eye, and they're looking to work with highly ethical organizations," Norris said. "When they work with us, they know they won't run into any moral or safety issues because our actions back up our core beliefs and theirs."

Values help leaders and employees hold each other accountable in a neutral yet meaningful way and instill a shared pride across all levels. Clearly defined and lived values can help you make difficult decisions, especially when numbers and analysis alone can't give you the answer or when there are shades of gray.

Here are five steps to help develop a values-driven culture:

1.  Collaboratively identify the right values for your organization.

2.  Define the behaviors that support each of your values.

3.  Get the word out.

4.  Integrate with organizational processes.

5.  Hold people and yourself accountable.

Let's expand on these steps.

### 1. Identify the Right Values for Your Organization

Values cards—cards that contain values statements—are a tool that can help you start the process of identifying core values in a fun and interactive manner. Many vendors sell them in decks ranging from twenty to thirty cards. Alternatively, you can do a computer search for a list of corporate values to use as a handout. Whichever method you choose, the approach is a simple process of elimination. The first step is to cut the list (or the number of cards) in half and then in half again. Continue the process until each team member has four to six "must have" values.

The sorting activity can be done individually or in teams. The final step is for the group to reach a consensus. During the consensus-building discussion, it is vital to consider the values against the previously agreed purpose statement. You want the values and the purpose statement to align well. Limiting the total number of values to four to six is also important. If your list is too long, they cannot all be core values and will represent too many priorities.

Once you have narrowed down the list, you are ready for some deeper discussion. Do these values truly resonate with everyone? Are there values not identified by this process that are core to your organization and the desired culture? Keep in mind that values rarely define what makes your organization unique. After all, many organizations have similar values. What they do is help you define, live, and sustain a unique culture. They are a way of specifying acceptable behavior and what you want to be known for. They guide you to make better business decisions and better people decisions.

## 2. Define Behaviors that Support Your Values

Many organizations rise admirably to the challenge of identifying their core values in a collaborative and thoughtful way. But this is just the first step because leaders must make sure these values are clearly defined and articulated in terms of behaviors and expectations. It is not enough to say that a key value is innovation. You need to define what you mean by innovation. What do innovative people do? How do they behave? Without such direction, it is nearly impossible to hold people accountable to the values you desire. Clarity is also critical for pinpointing the right talent fit, for recognizing and rewarding the right behaviors, and for overall sustainment of the culture you desire.

As with defining your organization's purpose, there are many ways to define the behaviors that support your values: draft them in a brainstorming session with the leadership team or employee groups; get input through internal social media; create an employee survey; hold focus groups; or use a combination of these methods. For example, Southwest Airlines is a farsighted company that, in 1990, established Culture Committees to inspire employees to own its legendary culture and strengthen and expand it geographically. Such committees are excellent vehicles for determining what your values mean.

As part of any discussion on values, consider what is critical to your organization in terms of where it is today and where it wants to be. Are there challenges you need to overcome? Behaviors that need to be changed? Value cards are an excellent starting point, but they can be rather generic.

For a specific example, let's turn to New Penn's Tom Collingsworth. Two years ago, New Penn rolled out new mission and core values statements that included wording on safety, integrity, accountability, change management, innovation, and shareholder value. "But safety is first and foremost," emphasizes Collingsworth. "We're not going to sacrifice safety just to make sure the customer gets their products. You can't have a safety culture unless you live and breathe it, and we have a president who does truly believe it—he doesn't pay lip service to it."

At New Penn, employees were encouraged to *not* perform a task if it was not safe, and supervisors were instructed to support them in this instead of pressuring them to take risks. As a result, safety metrics dramatically improved. But safety is not a value that often pops up in a set of value cards. So don't limit yourself to generic choices if there is a specific value that is critical to your organization.

### 3. Get the Word Out

No matter how much time you and your team invest in defining your values, if you do not put together a strategy to communicate the message, you will not successfully create the culture you want. Further, you need to think about communication in a multifaceted manner. Sir Winston Churchill believed that if you had a point to make, you should be direct, not subtle about it, and you should make that point numerous times. This is exactly what should be done with communicating corporate values. And this is another place where collaboration across levels and groups is important.

New Penn's Collingsworth said that the company used to operate with a top-down management approach. Communication and collaboration were not the forte. Now, he said, "We're trying to be more of a collaborative company, solicit employee's ideas, and make sure they have input on decision-marking. If you're a great communicator and willing to share information with employees, you can get so much more out of them."

The sample plan below will get you started on a company values communication plan. Note that no communication will be effective with a one-time or one-method approach. Create redundancies and ongoing repetition in your plan. Integrate discussion about your values into all your team meetings. Display them in print, on your intranet, and on your social media. Decide who in your organization is most important to enlist to spread the word. Are they your directors? Human Resources? Do you have an employee communications group? Can your marketing team help? Ideally, the CEO will be the messenger-in-chief.

### XYZ Company Communications Plan

| Action | Who | Timing |
|---|---|---|
| Town hall meetings led by CEO and other executives | CEO | Quarterly |
| Values listed and defined in a conspicuous place on the company intranet | Communications Team | Highlight a new value monthly |
| Posters of the values hung in breakrooms, etc. | Executive Assistant | Monthly |
| Talking points PowerPoint for department managers and HR Business Partners | Human Resources Communications Manager | Quarterly, following town hall meetings |
| Employee contest on what values mean to them with the winner selected by Employee Committees | Human Resources/Culture Committee | Quarterly |
| Train managers and employees the values and their associated behaviors | Human Resources (consider using an outside vendor to design and/or deliver the training) | Quarterly |

## 4. Integrate with Organizational Processes

Along with building an initial communications plan to showcase your values, it's critical that you develop a plan to integrate the values into your organizational processes. The time and energy you spend developing and articulating your purpose and values is wasted if you don't align your organization with them. Visionary, successful organizations spend much more time on this alignment than on crafting perfect statements and value definitions.

Begin by talking with your employees and customers about your core values. Ask them what gets in the way of living them. For example, let's say innovation is a core value. If employees are punished when they make a mistake, how much innovation are you going to see? In that example, punishment would be a deterrent to living the value of innovation. Perhaps a core value is respect for the individual, yet you have developed a complex approval and sign-off process for purchasing office supplies. This is not only cumbersome but also impedes decision-making and makes the individual feel he is not trusted. Eventually, such processes take on a mind of their own, to the point where no one remembers why they exist.

So how do you determine if your processes are aligned? First off, identify those that are not aligned. Create a few cross-functional work groups with six to eight people in each one. Give them a copy of your values and definitions and ask each group to identify four examples of processes that are misaligned with the values. Chances are, these groups will identify many of the same processes. You now have your low-hanging fruit. Start with changing these.

Whenever a team or department comes up with a new process, ask them to hold up the values mirror. Ask some key questions:

- What problem is this new process trying to solve?
- What is the cause of that problem?
- Will this new process eliminate that cause?

- What improvements do the new process offer us?
- How does this process impact customers?
- Which of our core values are impacted by this process? Are any negatively impacted?
- Is there a better way?

Leaders also need to own this process. At every executive retreat, take time to review four to six new processes or policies that were implemented or are about to be implemented. Ask the questions listed above. Have a frank and open discussion, and identify which processes need to be reworked.

## 5. Hold People and Yourself Accountable

Enron is an extreme example of an organization that did not hold itself or its team members accountable to the values they purported to have. For values to have meaning, they must be lived. They must be considered with every business and people decision that is made, even when that decision is costly or painful.

As Paul Stout, an IT director with a privately held global firm, bluntly told me, "If you're going to create values, you have to be willing to embody them."

Many years ago, one of our own team members was the head of human resources for a multi-state manufacturing company. One of her employees approached her with a very serious charge of sexual harassment. The charging employee's boss, a vice president and company officer, had hinted at career advancement in exchange for sexual favors. He was also threatening to fire one of her colleagues to reduce headcount while promising to keep her on. This led to an extensive, months-long investigation in which other unethical behaviors were uncovered. Many employees and the vice president himself were interviewed extensively, and the body of evidence continued to grow.

But this boss was a top producer and had the respect of the board and other executives. Our colleague and her boss, the general manager of their business unit, became extremely frustrated with the time it was taking the executive leadership team to reach an appropriate decision. At one point, the GM told our colleague, "After all we have heard and seen, if they do not fire this guy, I'm going to have to quit." That was an example of a leader living his own values.

Finally, the time for a decision arrived. The GM and my colleague presented their findings on a conference call with the executive team, including the CEO. A couple of the executives were concerned about firing the misbehaving VP because of the key role he played in the company. One suggested transferring him to another division across the country. The debate continued for a few minutes. Then the CEO interrupted. "I think this discussion has gone on long enough. Does this man support our values?" There was dead silence. "He does not. Not in any manner. He is fired. And I do not care if he is an officer. He is fired without severance. Tomorrow. Bring him in and tell him our decision."

This CEO demonstrated a deep and resounding commitment to his organization's values. The colleague who shared this story said, "This happened fairly early in my career, about seventeen years ago. I remember it like it was yesterday, and I always will. I will always hold that CEO and my GM in the deepest regard."

It takes courage to make painful decisions that honor your core values. But if you do not, employees will not trust your leadership. Leaders need to model personal work behaviors in accordance with the values they say they espouse.

---

Purpose and values are the essence of your company's identity and provide numerous advantages when you are trying to build or rebuild your culture. They make it easier to make tough decisions, to educate clients on what you stand for, and to identify the right employees for your organization. Our business environment today is extremely competitive, and defining who you are and what you stand for give you a competitive advantage.

# Diagnose

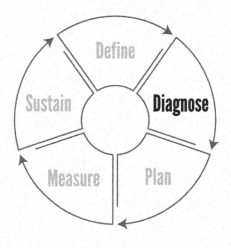

*If you don't understand the culture of your company, even your most brilliant strategies will fail. Your vision will be resisted, plans won't get executed properly, and all kinds of things will start going wrong.*
–Isadore Sharp, CEO, Four Seasons Hotels

It's no secret that competition has intensified in every industry, and no company is immune. Many companies are strong at execution, but this competency is no longer the top factor that determines success. Peter Drucker was perhaps more visionary than he ever imagined when he stated that culture eats strategy for breakfast.

The speed of change is an important consideration. Not only must we diagnose our culture thoroughly, we need to do it often. Not too many years ago, organizational shifts occurred at a measured pace. Company owners and executives had time on their side to identify patterns when a company plateaued, diagnose the causes, and plan cures. That luxury of time to investigate a corporate plateau and deeply probe why employees are mired in place no longer exists.

To spring forward, it's essential to implement a unique culture that's carefully aligned with the company's business strategy and values. It takes serious commitment and investment of time and resources to develop such a culture, but the impact is strikingly clear. A strong and targeted culture (like the Trader Joe's example given earlier) is hard to imitate. The competition can always copy *what you do*. It is much harder to emulate *who you are*. For this reason alone, a solid diagnosis of your culture is crucial. As Peter Drucker also said, "What gets measured gets managed." Before you can enhance or change your culture, you need to see it and understand it.

Of course, it's hard for leaders to assess their organization's culture and understand something in which they're immersed on a daily basis. An apt analogy is the familiar fable of the frog being boiled alive by putting it in tepid water and slowly bringing the water to boil. Because the temperature change is so gradual, the frog does not perceive danger. Eventually, it is cooked to death. Fortunately for frogs everywhere, this is only fable and not scientific fact. But it is an excellent metaphor for the human tendency to adjust and become dangerously complacent with our environment, to reach a plateau and stick there—until it's too late.

Before we explore the "diagnose" step in depth, let's take a look at what one large company did that was anything but a boiled-frog-complacent approach.

## Diagnosing What Your Organization Needs

In the food and beverage market there aren't many names bigger than the $19 billion Kraft Foods Group, Inc. And when you get that big, it's all too easy to plateau and lose sight of what drove your success in the first place. Bureaucracy can stifle growth and innovation and slow down all aspects of the business.

In 2012, Kraft tackled this issue head-on. Its solution was to split into two new companies: Kraft Food Groups, Inc., which would handle the North American grocery business, and a new entity, Mondeléz International, Inc., refocused as an international snack and confection company. Kraft Foods housed big-name brands such as Oscar Mayer, Planters, Velveeta and Jell-O; Mondeléz took products such as Trident and Oreo.

Tony Vernon, CEO of the new Kraft entity, brilliantly summed up their new strategy. "We will create a new Kraft, one with the spirit of a startup and the soul of a powerhouse." His goal was "nothing short of creating a renaissance in North American food and beverage."

Diane Leeming, who was Senior Director of Organization Development at Kraft at the time of the split, remembers that one impetus for the change was the bureaucracy that had slowed down growth. "There was too much red tape. Kraft had a problem getting products to market on a timely basis. Our competition might have had the same product idea and got it on the shelves while we were still in R&D."

The new, smaller (though still huge) company had a startup mentality with the funding and branding a startup never has. And because they were smaller, they could rally employees and be both nimbler and more creative.

As part of the "new Kraft," Vernon pledged that the company would move from a culture built on entitlement to a lean, horizontal organization in which layers of management would be eliminated, thereby removing the obstacle of having to rely on headquarters for direction and answers. And while the bureaucratic walls were being pulled down, so too were physical walls at the company headquarters in the Chicago suburb of Northfield. Open plan workspaces were created to reflect the new transparent and communicative environment. As Vernon so colorfully expressed it, "The stately cherry paneling of our previous executive offices will soon be history."

Kraft's stock subsequently soared, and the company was bought by Warren Buffett and merged with Heinz to create Kraft Heinz.

There are several approaches to gaining the required understanding of your existing culture, ranging from informal observations to in-depth, formal culture assessments. For the most thorough, accurate diagnosis, I recommend the research concept called triangulation, which simply means using more than one method (such as surveys, sales data, and focus groups) to collect information and data on the same topic. Triangulation also involves collecting information from more than one source. For example, collect information from multiple regions, business units, or levels of employees.

At the core, the purpose of your diagnosis is to determine alignment and authenticity. Consider the way you treat people, make decisions, and communicate. Consider how your office setting functions. Think about your written and unwritten rules. They all must authentically align with your purpose and values.

Culture diagnosis also requires you to examine your culture from multiple perspectives. Consider three levels of consciousness: facts, emotions, and symbols, as outlined in Ron Crossland and Boyd Clark's book *The Leader's Voice*. They are all heavily involved elements of culture change, and all three must be considered.

As you think about these three perspectives, refer to the diagram below to help you develop a multifaceted approach. Facts are primarily captured in policies, operating procedures, internal systems and control, and organizational structure. Emotions are captured in purpose, values, communication style, and code of conduct. Symbols come into play in the way offices are set up. Are they driven by position and level within the organization, or is there a sense of equality in the office design? Is collaboration between team members encouraged by the office design, or does it favor individuals working alone?

### Culture Diagnosis Diagram

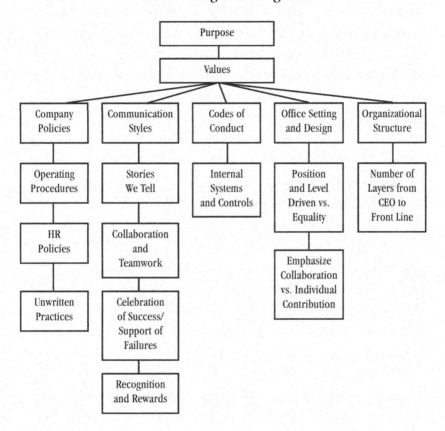

## Observation

Diagnosing your culture begins with observation. Below, I provide more insight into the process of observation as well as a variety of tools you can employ to gather information to make an effective diagnosis.

Observation is challenging because it requires you to become impartial. First, try to look at the employees and their interactions with each other and with customers through the eyes of an outsider. Start with your executives. Are they accessible? Do they interact with all levels of employees? What are their offices like? Are they all located on the top floor or in a separate wing of the office, segregated from the rank and file to display their top dog positions in the hierarchy, or are they more employee-friendly?

One of my colleagues shared a story about a company she worked for. The company was planning an office move, and she was on the moving committee. The CFO was adamant that the executives have their own private wing, with a private entrance and their own restrooms—something that's often deeply resented by the workforce at large.

Compare the attitude of that CFO with that of Jack Dorsey, cofounder of Twitter, when he started the post-Twitter venture, Square. Dorsey's office was in the dead center of an open floor plan. It consisted of a navel-high table and a computer. Michael Bloomberg, who believes that transparency produces fairness, operates the same way. Bloomberg's midtown Manhattan office is open space, including the workstations of top-level executives. Even conference rooms are transparent, with walls of clear glass that block noise but do not obscure vision.

McDonald's new $250 million headquarters located in Chicago's up-and-coming West Loop neighborhood is another classic example. Designed with collaboration in mind, it features "work neighborhoods," which give staff the flexibility to pick the kind of environment that best suits their needs that day. There are open floor plans, huddle rooms, communal tables, individual workstations, private phone rooms, and individual lockers. There are also unassigned benches, couches, and cubicles, as well as cafe-like work spaces that encourage impromptu conversations and collaboration.

But even when companies say they want to make a culture change, actions often don't match words. One executive I know, tasked with making his organization less hierarchical, recommended removing the executive parking spots in front of the building. It was an idea senior management rejected out of hand. What they said they wanted and what they were willing to do were two entirely different things.

The VP of human resources for a large manufacturing company shared a similar experience. One of the executives came into her office, disturbed about the appearance of the cubicles in the main open space. He felt they were messy and disorganized. He told her to institute a policy that no one could hang personal pictures, signs, or other decorations because they made the area look inconsistent and unprofessional. "At first, I thought he was kidding," she told me. "When I realized he was serious, it took a significant amount of self-control to avoid either laughing at him or throwing him out of my office. I made it clear to him that unless there was something offensive, it would be very unkind—as well as unwise—to tell people they could not decorate their cubicles." She felt that having personal objects in their cubicles suggested that the cubicle occupants felt at home there, something she believed he should be happy about. She tactfully pointed out that his own corner office with huge windows and expensive furniture held framed family photos.

Clearly, the office design and related policies of a company communicate key aspects of its culture. Sometimes, though, the office design may have been inherited, or there may not be sufficient budget to make dramatic changes no matter how much they are needed or desired. Make whatever changes you can make. Use the observation checklist below to perform other assessments about your organization. Take regular culture walks around your building and see what you discover.

## Culture Walk Tool

| Indicator | Observations |
|---|---|
| **Management Interaction with Employees**<br>• Formal or informal?<br>• Only in the manager's office vs manager often on the floor?<br>• Senior managers speak with all levels of employees regularly vs. only through their direct reports?<br>• Open door environment vs. employees have to knock or make an appointment? | |
| **Engagement and Emotion**<br>• What are people excited about?<br>• Are they laughing and energized?<br>• Are people morose or withdrawn?<br>• If you walk by desks, are people friendly and comfortable interacting with you and other ' senior leaders? | |
| **Objects and Artifacts on Desks and Walls**<br>• Desks/cubicles personalized?<br>• Meeting areas interactive or sterile?<br>• Family pictures or personal items on show?<br>• Plants, toys, or knickknacks displayed? | |
| **Allocation of Space**<br>• How much space is allocated to whom?<br>• Is employee position clearly delineated by furniture style or office size? | |
| **Displays and Common Areas**<br>• What is posted on bulletin boards?<br>• What kind of artwork is exhibited?<br>• How are common areas utilized?<br>• Are breakrooms used?<br>• Are breakrooms attractive and comfortable? | |
| **Communication and Interaction**<br>• Is there a sense of energy in the room?<br>• Do people talk with each other or communicate mostly by email?<br>• Is email typically formal or informal?<br>• Is hierarchy clearly delineated by where people sit in conference rooms?<br>• How much do you see people speaking with each other? What is their tone?<br>• Are people talking and laughing?<br>• Do people suddenly get quiet because you or another leader walks by? | |

# Culture Interviews

The process of digging into the corporate culture is called culture interviewing. Some organizations call these skip interviews or employee focus groups, but the process is the same. A director, vice president, or other senior leader holds a conversational session with her direct report's reports or any group of rank and file employees. Group size typically ranges from about eight to fifteen. You want enough people to generate engaged conversation but not so many that some of the more reticent employees feel uncomfortable speaking up.

The purpose of these interviews is to learn more about the culture of the work groups and the organization as a whole. As you listen, be sure to observe body language, facial expression, and tone of voice. You might want to have someone (an assistant or human resources employee, for instance) take notes, leaving you free to focus on interacting with employees and maintaining interaction eye contact. It's important that you lead the discussion and let your scribe take care of the note-taking. Here are two different approaches to asking questions.

### Start, Stop, Continue

- What are some things we can start doing to make this a better place to work?
- What are some things we should stop doing?
- What are some things we should continue doing?

### Culture Interview

- What would you tell a friend about our organization if they were about to start working here?
- What is the one thing you would most like to change about this organization?
- Who is a hero around here? Why?

- What is your favorite characteristic about our company?
- What is one thing you would change here if you could?
- What kinds of people would be most successful here?
- What kinds of people would likely not be successful here?

Regardless of the approach you take or the questions you ask, always make participants feel their contribution matters and let them know what you did with their input. Hold a follow-up session two to three months later to share with them which ideas were adopted, which were not and why, and which are being worked on.

## Employee Surveys

Organizations that want to grow their business and optimize their results inevitably realize they need to be looking inward to understand what's going on with their people. After all, business success starts and ends with people. Surveys are a practical and measurable way to gather valuable information from a large number of people in a short period of time. Such surveys also create valuable baseline data to ascertain progress as you move forward.

Three of the most widely used surveys are engagement, culture, and employee satisfaction surveys. Although related, they are not interchangeable. You want to be clear on the major differences between them. You may want to use one or all, with culture and engagement surveys being the more useful for this purpose. Let's look at the respective merits of each.

### Culture Surveys

Culture surveys provide you with indispensable information about the collective experience of your employees. Herb Kelleher, the former CEO of Southwest Airlines, once said, "Culture is what people do when no one is looking." So you need to look by asking. A simple way to think about culture surveys is that they provide the "we" perspective—this is how we do things around here. Although statements on culture surveys may be responded to using a rating scale (for example, a scale of 1-5), true/false answers are more often used. Whether you use true/false answers or a rating scale, these are examples of typical statements made:

- In our organization, we consider team results to be more important than individual results.

- In our organization, employees are encouraged to speak frankly to leaders, even when they disagree with the leader's opinion.

- In our organization, it is very important to closely follow policies and procedures.

Culture surveys are particularly useful when you are trying to change vision or strategic direction. They help you understand if employees are committed to and aligned with your organizational values. They are also useful to see differences across acquired companies or to determine employee perception after a merger. A culture survey enables organizations to understand the behaviors currently expected of people, discern the impact of the culture on its members, and establish a direction for cultural change efforts when an organization wants to create a culture that drives superior performance. The results from your organizational culture assessment will either confirm the efficacy of the culture you have or provide the direction for change.

### Engagement Surveys

Engagement surveys take an "I" perspective. Engagement measures an individual employee's emotional and intellectual connection and commitment to the company. They target employees' feelings about their day-to-day work experience, their managers, and leadership.

Engaged employees use greater discretionary effort in all they do. They are more productive, motivated, innovative, and creative, and they take more ownership of results. Engagement surveys typically measure and rank employee feelings using a scale, such as Five=Always, Four=Usually, 3= Sometimes, 2=Rarely, and 1=Never. Below are sample statements suitable for an engagement survey.

- I would recommend our company to friends and colleagues as a great place to work.

- My manager cares about me as a person.

- I have the opportunity to do what I'm best at every day.

- I have confidence that senior leadership is taking our organization in the right direction.

- I have the tools I need to do my job.

Engagement surveys are helpful to develop strategies to enhance performance, reduce turnover, and improve the workplace. Employees who are highly engaged are more likely to provide better customer service and be more focused on achieving company objectives. ISS, a provider of global facility services, surveyed over 2,500 clients, and after analyzing over 500,000 employee responses to an engagement survey, found a very high correlation between employee engagement and customer satisfaction.[20] For decades, Gallup has also reported that there is a strong relationship between employee engagement and customer satisfaction.

You can purchase off-the-shelf surveys, work with a vendor to semi-customize your surveys, or custom design surveys yourself. Each approach has a few pros and cons, but in general, I recommend that clients use experienced vendors who will customize some of the questions. For example, you should develop questions specifically around the new or revised values your organization came up with during the "define" phase because you will want to know how widely lived those values are and what gaps you need to fill.

In addition, experienced vendors will have data you can use to compare your company's results to those of companies that are similar to yours in size and industry. And writing survey questions that are reliable and validated is not easy. A good vendor will simplify and automate the survey and reporting process for you, provide analysis of the results, provide recommendations and solutions, and help ensure confidentiality to better ensure honest answers from your employees. A good vendor will also help you develop spot surveys so you can stay abreast of changes and trends over short periods of time.

Culture and engagement are linked, and they certainly impact each other. No matter which surveys you choose—and it is often valuable to do both—don't forget to share the results with your employees, involve them in improvement strategies, and hold managers accountable for improvement.

### *Employee Satisfaction Surveys*

Employee satisfaction surveys, also called employee opinion surveys, are valuable for general feedback to management and human resources. They cover topics such as job satisfaction, perception of pay and benefits, key causes of turnover, perception of policies, opportunities for advancement and, at times, even perception of human resources itself. Sometimes they're confused with engagement surveys, but their focus is much more on the specifics of pay, benefits, and other issues typically managed by human resources. They might round out your accumulated knowledge of your work environment, but they're not particularly targeted to acquire meaningful insight into your culture. I mention them mainly to clarify any potential confusion among common survey types.

As with culture interviews, it's vital to share all survey results with employees in a timely manner. And let me repeat, be sure to involve all levels of employees in planning what to do with the information you have gathered. Diagnosing your culture is an important step. It is the foundation for developing strategies and plans to improve your culture, which is the next step in the process.

## Diagnosing Your Processes and Policies

As you go through the process of diagnosing your current culture, it is not enough to determine how your employees perceive your culture and whether your office setting supports your new vision. You also want to examine overall alignment of your general policies, processes, and practices. I recommend starting with policies and processes that are written down because those will be easier to treat concretely.

Begin by selecting the right team of employees to tackle this task. Often, policies and processes outlive their value and purpose. The team you put together will want to weed those out and hold them up to the values test. In other words, do they support the values and new vision for your culture or are they a barrier? Are they conflicting? Here are some tips to get you started.

- Create a balanced team of people, to include those who are very familiar with the policies or practices that you are evaluating and those who are unfamiliar with them. The experienced employees will know which policies are rigorously applied and why. The unfamiliar folks will be able to challenge the processes and not simply assume they are needed because you have always done things that way. As with the "define" phase, it is helpful to get input from multiple levels of employees as you examine your processes and policies.

- Keep the group small. A maximum of six to eight works well. If you have a lot of documented policies and procedures, you may end up with two or three different teams.

- Prioritize your approach. Start with policies that are suspect or already known to be problematic. Alternatively, begin with the policies that have the broadest impact on the largest numbers of people.

- Use the discussion template below as a guide.

**Process and Policy Review Discussion Guide**

| Purpose Statement | Values | Key Behaviors Supporting the Values | Processes and/or Policies to Be Reviewed | Discussion Points and Issues |
|---|---|---|---|---|
| | 1. | | | |
| | 2. | | | |
| | 3. | | | |
| | 4. | | | |
| | 5. | | | |
| | 6. | | | |

# Diagnosing Recognition and Rewards

Companies that show appreciation to their employees reap the rewards of higher engagement and increases in the behaviors they want to see. Some of the behaviors you definitely want to see more of are those you related to your values. Recognizing employees for living your values is necessary to reinforce them and inspire people to take them to heart.

Jennifer Speciale, Executive Recruiter, Global Lead for Experience Design, McKinsey Design at McKinsey & Company, told me, "Recognition comes in different ways besides a pat on the back or a raise. It's about allowing people to work on a new project, or involving them in a cross-functional team, or recognizing their value by giving them a little more responsibility. Nothing makes employees feel more trusted or valued than the opportunity to prove themselves to the boss and their associates."

She also recommends that you invest in your employees by making access to continuing education easier for them, giving them a mental health day to recharge their batteries, and donating in their name to a worthy cause of their choice. "With the increase of purpose-driven work from the millennial generation, companies that embrace this type of recognition incentive perpetrate the type of company culture many seek today."

Recognizing solid efforts, whether fruitful or otherwise, helps build long-term loyalty and success. Don't just celebrate success, celebrate failure, as long as something has been learned. Small win, big win—it doesn't matter. What does matter is the little ways you can give accolades to your team members to boost their spirits and keep them motivated to achieve future wins.

Frequency of rewards and recognition is another important aspect of driving culture change. Traditional employee of the year (and even employee of the month) programs are not frequent or varied enough to reinforce the behavioral shift you are looking for.

Here is a simple tool you can apply to determine if your rewards and recognition strategies are in line with your desired culture:

**Diagnosing Your Recognition and Reward Programs and Strategies**

| Values | Way Currently Recognized or Rewarded | Frequency | Current Impact | Gaps |
|--------|--------------------------------------|-----------|----------------|------|
| 1. | | | | |
| 2. | | | | |
| 3. | | | | |
| 4. | | | | |
| 5. | | | | |
| 6. | | | | |

Diagnostics are essential. Don't assume you have a deep and clear understanding of your culture. A thorough diagnosis is an essential step in the process of moving your organization off the plateau. Diagnosing requires multiple approaches and the involvement of your employees. You want to get as complete a picture of your current state as you can. Only then will you be able to develop plans that will help drive the culture shift you seek.

# Planning: Strategy and Process Alignment

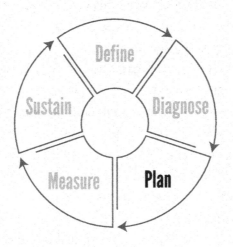

*Culture shift occurs when the targeted culture perfectly aligns with the business strategy and values, not when they sort of align.*
–Emmett Vaughn, Director, Office of Diversity
and Engagement, Exelon

Getting your strategy and processes in alignment is an essential undertaking that enables you to deliver value to customers and stakeholders. Your strategy articulates your organization's overall goals and the key tactics to achieve them, and business processes guide the way to accomplishing them. It's a hand-in-glove endeavor. You can't have one without the other—assuming you want to be successful.

Why do organizations need formal processes? Let's look first at startups. Leaders of new companies wear many different hats. They're usually too busy getting the business off the ground and moving too fast to standardize their processes, let alone document them. The focus is more on making things happen than worrying about the *right steps* to make them happen. As a result, the development of formal processes takes a backseat, as well as the systems that are essential for improving customer satisfaction and enhancing the company's ability to react to rapid market change. This can be a serious delinquency because these systems and processes are also vital for organizations to scale effectively as they grow.

What about established organizations? They face a very different problem. Their processes are often deeply engrained, and they may have failed to keep pace with changing market demands, technology, and customer expectations. The processes may have outlived their value, but they are still followed simply because there is a "we have always done it this way" mindset. Often, these organizations don't take into account the changing needs of their customers and realign their processes accordingly.

Other organizations spend a great deal of energy being overly focused—sometimes to the point of obsession—on the competition. While no company wants to be surprised by a competitor's out-of-the-box breakthrough initiative or a new competitor totally disrupting the industry, it is important to keep your eyes sharply trained on the customer first. "If you're competitor-focused, you have to wait until there is a competitor doing something. Being customer-focused allows you to be more pioneering," says Jeff Bezos, CEO of Amazon, succinctly making the point.

One of the biggest process problems I see in many organizations is a siloed approach to executing the work. Most organizations are structured around time-honored functions such as operations, human resources, sales, marketing, production, and finance. The problem with structuring functional units like these is that they can be detrimental to overall organizational performance. In fact, in some companies, functional units may even work against each other. This is especially common when the leaders of functional units place the needs of their own unit ahead of the needs of the organization as a whole or ahead of the needs of the customer.

But what does this have to do with culture? Everything! First, reflect on your organization's purpose and strategy. Your purpose is all about why you exist and what you hope to achieve. Your strategy articulates how you will get there. Ask yourself how well your strategy supports your purpose.

Next, consider your culture. If your culture does not encourage and facilitate collaboration and information sharing (as opposed to information hoarding), if business units are rewarded primarily for business unit performance (as opposed to organizational success), or if you lack a culture of continuous improvement, your processes will not be aligned. Your customers—and ultimately, your business—will suffer.

As you think about your culture and how well it supports your ability to develop well-aligned processes, look at your deep-seated beliefs about both customer experience and employee experience. Ask yourself four questions, and ask them often:

- Does each of your processes exist for a reason, or are you asking employees to just check the box?

- Have you talked with your customers across the entire life cycle of the relationship?

- What are they telling you works, doesn't work, and needs to change?

- What is the quality of your employees' experiences with your internal processes?

Brian Chesky, cofounder and CEO of Airbnb, insists that culture is vital to businesses because when the culture is strong, people can be trusted to do the right thing, and fewer processes are needed. So what does that mean? It means that the business is probably more efficient and effective, as well as a happier place for people to work.

Processes are developed by people, executed by people, and ignored by people. So let's start there. Customer-centric companies give employees the authority (and accountability) to act to address customers' needs at the point of contact. Employees need to be able to make judgments and quickly solve problems for customers without multiple levels of approval or review.

This approach is exemplified by Ritz-Carlton, whose motto, "We are ladies and gentlemen serving ladies and gentlemen," is supported by a variety of guidelines and an emphasis on employee development. Ritz Carlton has realized that when employees are knowledgeable and well-trained and when they have the right service orientation, they are going to make the right decisions for the customer.

In my mind, this deep level of trust helps inspire even better decision making. But more than that, employees need to know they will not be punished or chastised if they do something other than standard procedure, especially if it was the right decision for the customer. If failing to follow procedures or challenging them when they impede the customer experience results in punishment, what do you expect will happen? At the very least, the organization will become stagnant. At worst, it will be left in the dust by businesses that have a corporate culture that fosters trust.

Keeping your purpose and focus simple is another important component for effective employee empowerment. Auto Club of Southern California's Chris Baggaley says that he has seen organizations make their purpose and focus unnecessarily complex. In contrast, the Auto Club philosophy is simple: "We exist for our members, to keep our members for life." From this foundation, it is simple to cascade the approach throughout financial metrics, growth metrics, processes, and all other aspects of business.

Baggaley points out that culture can even vary within an organization across the country. "You can't assume that because something is successful in one place, it will automatically be successful in another. You can't just transpose the culture in one region without appreciating that there are significant nuances elsewhere." How can you overcome that challenge? "You've got to have an overarching culture, but you need to recognize the need for subcultures." One way to do this is to cross-pollinate people and cultures.

We don't inspire people when we ask them to not think and just follow instructions. But when you empower people, you make everyone a change agent.

As you work to ensure alignment between your culture and your processes, stop focusing so much on the processes. Instead, think about those employees who interact with the customer and what happens in that interaction. Tell them to remove the processes from the equation and to concentrate on meeting the needs of the customer. What would it be like if that was their sole purpose? How would they design the work then?

Wait a minute. No processes? How can we work without processes? What would happen to consistency? How could we hold people accountable? To clarify, I'm not referring to process steps. Rather, I am suggesting a mindset shift in which you ask employees what they would do if they had the freedom and flexibility to do whatever they wanted, whatever made the most sense for the customer. This goes beyond the everyday routine, and it has the possible impact of reinvigorating them with the same passion and enthusiasm for the business that they had on day one.

An annual employee engagement study from The Temkin Group, a customer experience research, consulting, and training firm, highlights the significance of engaged employees. Its 2016 report showed that companies that excel at customer experience have one-and-a-half times as many engaged employees as customer experience laggards.[21] Time and again, other studies have supported this concept. "On average, employees are three times more engaged in world-class companies than they are in middle-of-the-road organizations," says ADP's Andrew Koehler. It is an important data point to keep in mind.

## Employee Experience Mapping Tool

It can be challenging to look at your processes with a neutral, independent eye. Many of them have been in place for quite some time and may be taken for granted. To determine if the processes that touch your employees are aligned with the culture you think you have or the culture you would like to have, there's a helpful process tool called Employee Experience Mapping. Here's how it works:

### 1. Form the Team

Any employee can be part of this process. After all, they all have first-hand knowledge of most of the typical employee experiences at your organization. That being said, here are some tips to aid in the selection of team members:

*Diversity:* Think broadly here. Look at age, gender, department, tenure, level, region, business unit, and so on. You want a broad perspective. Sure, your HR team is most familiar with your employee experiences and processes, but they might also be defensive or protective of the policies they put in place. Additionally, they might be more focused on what makes their jobs easier or more efficient than what provides a better experience for the employees. So make sure you cast a wide net to gather input.

*Size:* Consider having about sixteen people on the team so you can break them up into smaller work groups and get varied and balanced opinions.

*Inspiration:* In general, you want people who will be excited about being part of this process. It might be tempting to shy away from the "troublemakers," but those folks can contribute important perspectives. Balance them with people who have natural leadership ability and a passion for the company. This could also be a stimulating project for some of your high potential employees.

## 2. Set the Stage

Fire them up! Get people excited about the project. Give them the big picture view of what you are doing and why. Be careful to lay down some ground rules so there are no misunderstandings and so you can stay on course in a productive manner. Typical ground rules would be respecting each other's opinions, being a good listener, and looking for solutions rather than complaining. I like to have teams set their own ground rules. Those I provide here are merely starting point examples.

## 3. Brainstorm Common Employee Experiences

The group should begin by brainstorming a list of the most common employee experiences. These include things like the job application processes, onboarding, learning and development, benefits enrollment, performance management, career planning, promotion, pay increase, and retirement. From this list, teams pick three to five processes that touch the most employees or that most members of the group regard as particularly problematic. Also consider which processes are the most poorly aligned with your culture and business strategy. For example, if one of your values is to promote from within but your employee job posting process is cumbersome or seldom leads to internal promotions, you have a misaligned policy or practice. If a key business strategy is to be known for automation and ease of use but your benefits enrollment process is highly manual, then your employee experience is misaligned, and employees know it all too well. Employee frustration translates into how they interact with customers. Practice what you preach!

### 4. Develop Personas

Once you've identified the initial key processes, develop a few persona backgrounds. Personas are fictitious characters you create to portray the employee experience. Give them a name, a job title, an age, years of service, and a brief role description. Think typical demographics of your employee base or perhaps different business units or regions. This step has several advantages. First, processes are often *not* experienced the same way in all locations or by all levels of employees. For example, your onboarding process might be very different in the field versus in the corporate office. Second, when you create personas, it allows people to see the process from a personal point of view. Here are two simple persona examples:

May Lee: Customer Service Rep
Location: Chicago Service Center
Age: 32
Years with Company: 6
May is a customer service rep. Her primary role is to answer email and phone inquiries from our members. She works on a team of fifteen reps and typically handles fifty to seventy-five calls a day. She is measured on talk time and problem resolution.

Leslie Whitney: Web Developer
Location: San Francisco Data Center
Age: 45
Years with Company: 4

Leslie is a web developer. His primary role is to develop customer-facing, highly engaging product websites. He works on a team of twelve. He is directly measured on customer ratings about the site, and indirectly on sales volume generated by the site.

## 5. Map the Processes

Now you are ready to start mapping the process from your employee personas' points of view. You might want each team to map the same process from a different persona point of view. Employees jot down each step in the process on sticky notes and place them on a wall in the order in which the steps occur. In doing this, they quickly recognize any missed steps that can be easily added. The teams can also visually identify where different personas might have different employee experiences. Here is an example of what these sticky notes might look like for an Employee Job Posting process from May's point of view.

### Employee Job Posting Process

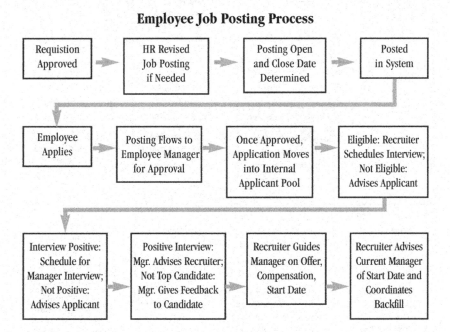

## 6. Look for Breakdown Points and Improve the Process

Once the processes are mapped out, team members should look for redundancies and bottlenecks and start to streamline the process. They can use different colored sticky notes for direct employee touchpoints, for values misalignments, for bottlenecks, and for both positive and negative experiences. This gives an at-a-glance frame of reference. Then the team can develop alternative approaches and solutions. Once the team has a potential solution, it needs to come up with a pilot or test plan to see if the new process is truly a significant improvement. If it is, then they need to develop a plan to implement it. Here is an example of the above employee job posting process marked up for potential bottlenecks, critical employee touchpoints, or values misalignments.

### Employee Job Posting Process

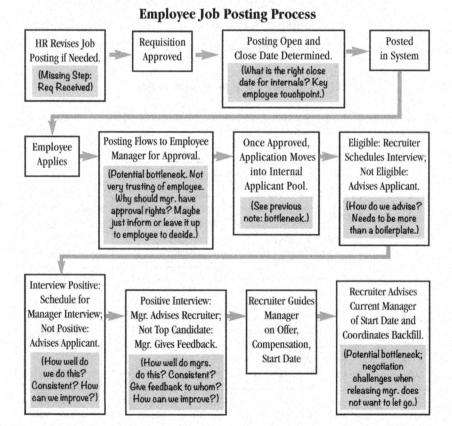

This process is a powerful way to involve employees across functions and multiple levels to enhance the employee experience and therefore your culture in a very concrete way. It gives you exciting and valuable insight into what they think and how they want to make things better. As Ernest Hemingway once said, "I like to listen. I have learned a great deal from listening carefully. Most people never listen."

## Customer Experience Mapping Tool

In companies that put an emphasis on seamless customer interaction, such interaction is consistent—whether the staff responds to customer emails or greets them in person. None of this harmonious, holistic approach happens by chance or accident. The companies that excel in customer interaction only perform so flawlessly because they have invested heavily in researching and designing the optimum customer journey.

The Customer Experience Mapping Tool has many similarities with Employee Experience Mapping, but I have highlighted some differences.

### 1. Form the Team

Your initial thought might be to put together a team that only consists of those employees who directly interface with the customer, such as sales reps and customer service reps. But this will not give you a complete perspective. Keep in mind that customers are not always the people who buy your product. They are not always the end consumer. If you are vertically integrated, customers might be other business units. You should also include employees who are upstream in the process—for example, order pickers in the warehouse, or delivery drivers, or product designers. If possible, add some customers to the team.

### 2. Set the Stage

As with the steps for employee experience mapping, get people excited about the project. Outline the big picture objective. Clearly state what you are doing and why. Set ground rules.

### 3. Identify Your Different Customer Types and Initial Touchpoints

Your customers are not all alike—except for the one thing they have in common, which is being your customer. Your types of customers can be very simple or quite complex, depending on your business and industry. Think channels, account size, regions, or products, depending on what makes sense for your business. Begin by listing your different types of customers in a matrix. Then think about all the different types of media they use to interact with you. The sample matrix below for a cabinet manufacturing company is an example that will help you create a version that can be tailored for your business.

**Typical Initial Touchpoint with Company**

| Type of Customer | Website | Kitchen Designer | Showroom | Account Manager |
|---|---|---|---|---|
| Consumer | X | X | X | |
| Home Builder | | | | X |
| Lumber Yard | | X | | X |
| Cabinet Dealer | X | X | | X |

### 4. Develop Personas

Once you've identified your customer types, develop personas for each type, just as you did for your various employee types. You should also tap in to notes from customer focus groups and customer surveys to round out your personas. Be sure to involve your customer service and sales teams. After all, who knows your customers better than they do?

### 5. Identify Key Touchpoints for Each Customer Persona

Customers interact with any organization from a variety of touchpoints. Make a map for each of the customer types and the typical interactions. The flow chart below gives you some ideas about what to consider. There might be touchpoints missing or ones that do not apply to your organization, so simply adjust accordingly. Keep in mind that you have many touchpoint experiences. For example, returns and late deliveries are both touchpoints.

**Example of Start-to-Finish Customer Touchpoint Experience**

- *Interest:* How the customer becomes aware of your product or service (advertisement, word-of-mouth/referral, sales representative, etc.)

- *Research:* How the customer learns more about your product (company website, consumer website, call to customer service or sales rep, store visit, etc.)

- *Purchase:* How the customer pays for your product (in person, online, purchase order, credit card, etc.)

- *Delivery:* How the customer receives your product (pick up/will call, common carrier, UPS, USPS, etc.)

- *Installation:* How the customer sets up your product for use (independent installer, employee installer, self, etc.)

Now you are ready to start to map the processes in detail. You will map them from your customer personas' points of view, just as you did for the employee experiences.

### 6. Look for Breakdown Points and Improve the Process

Once the processes are mapped out, team members can look for redundancies, pain points, and bottlenecks so they can start to streamline the process. This is when the team needs to think about how customers are feeling. The emotional aspect of the customer journey is as important as the logistical steps.

What are some of the emotional red flags? Where are the friction points? Is this a point where your persona is feeling delighted or frustrated? In other words, consider each customer's journey as a story. Stories help us personalize and internalize what is going on and make it easier to recognize patterns to the interactions. You are looking for insights into bottlenecks so you can truly optimize your customer's experience, regardless of the type of customer they are. A simple approach is to mark each step with an emoji indicating how the customer might feel about their experience.

## One Brick at a Time

I've talked about the concept of having a customer-centric approach. Now let's look at a company that has been successful in part because they have one.

In just six-and-a-half years, XL Catlin's North America Construction insurance business hit the $2 billion underwriting milestone. From zero to $2 billion in that timeframe is quite remarkable. Even more remarkable is that after reaching $1 billion, it only took the company another eighteen months to double its written premiums.

What kind of corporate culture stimulates such sustained and skyrocketing success? How did they manage to go beyond the plateau?

Division president Gary Kaplan says it started with "a big, hairy, audacious goal" to hit $1 billion in six years—a target it obviously surpassed. Kaplan and his team adopted a multi-faceted approach to business and culture development that included the following elements:

### Customer-centric

They first identified the need for an insurance carrier that had a genuine customer-centric focus, in contrast to most companies' focus on building internal efficiencies.

"One thing I've learned in my thirty-eight-year career is that while you can manage your business through projects, you can't treat your customers like projects," said Kaplan. "Instead, it's all about listening and learning from them and building long-term relationships." Kaplan calls it the "voice of the customer," and it's the foundation of their business model.

Obviously, this kind of relationship does not happen overnight. It takes time and the willingness to engage in a continuous improvement approach that can take years. "You need to dig in for the long haul and be willing to make disruptive changes in the day-to-day business operations that shift the focus entirely on the customer."

Done right, it builds trust and long-lasting, profitable customer relationships. "It requires taking actions to shift the mindset of your people, help them to think differently, and to see the customer as the center of their everyday work and processes. This means truly understanding the customer's business from a broad perspective, not just a specific insurance product perspective. The customers' priorities need to be our priorities."

### Finding and Developing the Right People

Implementing a customer-centric strategy requires finding the right people—something XL Catlin did from day one. The people they hired were those who fit on their team and could help forge lasting relationships with North America's top contractors.

Not only do the right people need to be hired, the people hired need to be developed. Kaplan created an Extended Leadership Team (ELT) to ensure development of a pipeline of talent, the next generation of leaders.

He emphasized the value of using the experience of longtime employees. "Don't let your most senior people retire before you pull out of their heads all of the value that they bring to the table, all of the knowledge they have acquired. Teach your seasoned people how to be teachers, and have them spend more time on that instead of their regular jobs."

### Culture of Change

XL Catlin uses ninety-day results-focused projects called Rapid Results Initiatives (RRIs), which are team-based, problem-solving, change-driving projects originally developed by Schaffer Consulting. "Having a ninety-day timeline for a project is the magic amount of time that keeps everyone excited and motivated," Kaplan said. "We decided that continuous improvement has to be one of our big cultural themes. It's something we are working hard to embed in the culture of the company."

### Planning

To accomplish continuous improvement, the company has adopted a leadership, planning and execution model in which they simultaneously have a structured way of planning the work and a structured way of working the plan. "As we're implementing it, we're already planning for the next year. You need sound operational planning. You have to prioritize—what's important versus what's urgent. Where do next year's projects fit into the priority versus the value?"

## Communication

Kaplan holds a monthly call for forty-five minutes in which everyone who is a part of the call participates. Presenters get five minutes for their update. "It forces them to become better communicators and not ramble on. The people who take part in the call feel like they own the results. They own the business."

Once a year, five basic teams, five profit centers of between fifteen and twenty-five people from all across the country, come together for an in-person meeting to give them the opportunity to get to know each other.

## Transparency and Teamwork

Kaplan believes that it is important to be transparent. A part of that transparency is showing everyone the numbers monthly, in the form of simple charts. He also believes that it is critical to have input from all levels of the organization. "Not only does it provide you with more diverse thinking, but also strengthens buy-in when it comes time to deliver. Look for opportunities that give people enough freedom and flexibility to be innovative."

## Time to Think

There is no question that companies need active, engaged employees. But does engagement mean constant busyness? "One thing we've learned from employee surveys is you need to give your team time to think, time to contemplate how they can make changes," Kaplan said. "If there's no slack in people's days, they can't do the things that make them more effective. Some people need time to meditate or exercise.

When you encourage them to take a break, it refreshes their brains and also helps foster a culture where they are willing to share information with others and generate momentum."

### Advance a Talent Culture

According to Kaplan, "You have to keep reinforcing to people the most important things: being accountable, doing what's right, being future-focused, collaborating, and making it better together. These are the behaviors that count to create the right culture."

––––––––––

Whether you are a startup or a well-established organization, processes are critical to efficiency and consistency. It is important not to neglect their development, but at the same time, we need to make sure they do not take on a life of their own. Your employee and customer experience processes need to be aligned with your strategy and your culture, and as you shift and change, they need to be revisited. Making sure your processes and both your customer and employee experiences are aligned with your organization's purpose, strategy, and culture will not happen by chance. Such alignment requires intentional planning and ongoing monitoring. The right processes drive engagement, which in turn helps attract and retain the right people. And nothing happens without the right people to make it happen.

# Planning: People Make It Happen

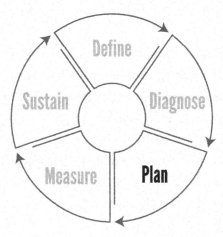

*Don't hire chess players and use them as chess pieces.*
–Bala Sathyanarayanan, Executive Vice President
of Human Resources, Xerox

We've all heard it a thousand times: Our people are our most important asset. But there are some issues with that mantra. Most companies don't act like they mean it, and their employees know it. And it isn't quite true anyway. Just having people in seats, on the road, or on the manufacturing floor will not make good things happen for you. You need the right people in those seats, on the road, and on the manufacturing floor. Once you have that, your people truly will be your most important asset.

How do you know you are hiring the right people, identifying the kinds of people you need well in advance of hiring them, onboarding them in the right way, developing them, and engaging them? How do you know you are recognizing them, rewarding them, and promoting them effectively? There is an entire ecosystem of people treatment—let's call this talent management—that you must do well to ensure you find and keep the right people. Because if you don't, nothing else really matters. Policies don't do the work, forms don't build rapport with your customers, and procedures do not solve problems. People do. The right people do. And the right people do not happen by accident or by luck.

It's amazing how much time and money organizations invest in their business planning, marketing strategies, financial management, and operational plan. It is equally amazing how little time and money they spend on their people strategies. Yet, unless you are a manufacturing firm with large investments in raw materials, the single biggest expense line on your P&L is probably your payroll. Yes, your people are your most expensive asset, but they are often the one that receives the least investment. It makes no sense. If you sub-optimize your talent, you will pay the price.

Earlier, I showed you a simple model to help you lead a critical culture shift. The Planning phase of this model is where definition and diagnosis meet the human element. You can do a fabulous job of thinking through your desired culture and defining your purpose and values. You can meticulously measure and honestly take stock of your gaps and challenges. But without a plan that is well thought out and intentional, your efforts all go to waste. Your people strategy—your talent management strategy—is the foundation for a healthy culture that will serve your organization well. You don't really have a culture strategy until you have the people aligned with that strategy. So ask yourself what kind of people you need to execute the strategy and how you get them.

Another theme I have often heard is to look for ways to flatten your organization. Think about how many levels there are between your CEO and the frontline employee. Bureaucracy is a culture and empowerment killer. Bala Sathyanarayanan told me how Xerox reduced thirteen layers between the CEO and the lowest level to seven layers. By having no employee more than six people away from the CEO, they created more effective communication in both directions. "This kind of environment is a veritable breeding ground for collaboration and innovation that was lacking when the organization had thirteen layers."

In 2016, Oracle conducted an extensive study on talent and its impact on culture. Specifically, it researched what it called "talent magnet" companies to discover what they did differently and the value that strong talent management practices could have on creating a positive culture. What they discovered was simple in theory but hard in practice. "Ultimately, talent organizations live their values. Without exception, each company created talent processes that perpetuated their stated values and purpose," the Oracle report stated.[22]

## What It Costs When You Don't Do It Well

What does this mean for you? Let's first take a look at some financial facts related to the costs of turnover and poor hiring choices.

### Turnover

Turnover costs are hard to precisely target. According to Josh Bersin, of Bersin by Deloitte, you need to consider a wide range of factors including the costs of hiring, onboarding (including training and management time), lost productivity, lost engagement, customer service errors, long-term training, and cultural impact. It's rare for organizations to be able to precisely track all these costs, which is why it's difficult to peg a hard number to the cost of turnover. Such data vary, but no matter which numbers you buy in to, the message is evident: Turnover is very expensive.

The Society for Human Resources Management (SHRM) provides some modest estimates. To replace someone holding a frontline, lower-paying job costs 16 percent of their annual salary. For example, it would take $3,328 to replace a $10.00 per hour full-time retail employee. To replace a midrange position such as a frontline supervisor whose annual salary is $40,000, the cost is 20 percent of that salary, or $8,000. For an executive, you're looking at up to 213 percent, so replacing a $200,000 leader would cost more than $400,000. Surprisingly, many executives are not aware of the hard numbers and the perspective they provide.

Dr. John Sullivan, an internationally-known talent thought leader, provides another perspective on the impact of turnover. When organizations suffer from high turnover, they are more likely to hire quickly and settle for average candidates. "If your company has a turnover of 20 percent per year and all of your new hires are mediocre, it will only take five years for all of your entire workforce to be mediocre."

One final thought about turnover. Employees do not quit because a great new job fell into their laps. Most people hate looking for jobs. It is a difficult, time-consuming, and painful process. So if an employee quits, you can assume someone did something (or several things) that drove them out the door. It could be their manager, company policies, or you. And it's up to you to figure out the patterns of disaffection and fix them.

### Poor Hire

According to SHRM, the cost of a poor hire ranges from $300,000 to $500,000 when you consider the errors such hires might make, the impact they have on their team and customers, and the time the manager has to spend addressing poor performance.

Dr. Sullivan has also reported that this bad hire cost can translate into as much as $7,000 per day as you work on replacing the person you just got rid of. Think about that. Every day that you or your managers postpone hiring decisions, the money clock is ticking, and ticking hard.[23]

## Engagement and Talent Strategies

According to a Gallup report on the relationship between engagement and organizational outcomes, the rate of efficiency at which most businesses operate because of poor engagement levels is 30 percent. How can that disappointing percentage be improved? Three key drivers of positive engagement are trust in senior leadership, relationship with the front-line supervisor, and the opportunity for learning and development.[24]

Andrew Koehler of ADP says that even world class organizations tend to lose 7 percent of productivity every day due to meetings, email, and a general lack of engagement. The impact for middle-of-the-road organizations is double: 15 percent. And for underperforming organizations, it is as much as 21 to 40 percent. Koehler told me, "It is monumental how often underperforming companies ignore the people side. They add levels of management to fix this, which just creates more bureaucracy."

What's a leader to do? First, stop paying lip service to the concept of people as an asset, not a cost, and truly think of them that way. And plan your talent strategies to attract and retain the best possible people you can. Work in partnership with your human resources team, who should be ahead of you in this process. If they're not, you might want to consider reevaluating the talent on that team first!

What do you need to know to help you attract and retain the right people? There are five essential people strategies: workforce planning; talent acquisition; onboarding; development; and performance management and coaching.

## *Workforce Planning*

Workforce planning is the process of identifying not only current talent needs but also future talent needs. Brian Becker, Mark Huselid, and Richard Beatty analyzed two decades of academic research for their book *The Differentiated Workforce*. They found that workforce strategy has to come first if a company wants competitive advantage.

Workforce planning allows us to pinpoint the roles that are critical to executing our business strategy, define the competencies and skills those jobs require, and determine whether our current incumbents meet those requirements. An added benefit to workforce planning is that it enables us not only to identify the key roles needed to execute our strategy but also to assess whether such roles even currently exist in our organization.

Identifying your strategic roles is an excellent way to think about people as assets. This approach allows you to target and invest your precious recruiting and training dollars wisely. And by the way, you and your leadership team are not strategic roles. This is not about who develops the strategy, it's about who executes it. Strategic roles can often be those performed by your frontline employees (you know, those employees who probably have the highest turnover and the lowest salary). Disney considers the role of street sweeper to be strategic, Southwest Airlines its flight attendants, FedEx its delivery drivers, and Google its software engineers. What are your strategic roles? Identify them and target them for your best acquisition and retention initiatives.

## *Talent Acquisition*

Talent acquisition is not merely hiring or filling open positions. As stated above, it needs to start with the strategic perspective that workforce planning provides. But you also need to look at what qualities are going to best fit your culture. An essential part of selection is ensuring a fit with your values. When you carefully define your values, you can more accurately assess whether a candidate is a good match.

Of course, your values—when lived—translate into your culture. For Tony Hsieh, CEO of Zappos, culture is the number one priority. "We decided that if we get the culture right, most of the stuff, like building a brand around delivering the very best customer service, will just take care of itself."[25] Getting the culture right is supported, instead of undermined, by acquiring talent that fits with it.

Employees whose values match those of their organization, their coworkers, and their supervisor typically are more engaged and more likely to remain with their organization, all of which should lead to better job performance. But as Charles Lilly of Hub International told me, you have to be transparent about what those values are and what your culture is like. "For example, we are a fast-paced and fast-growth company. This isn't for everyone. People need to know what to expect if they are going to come to work for us."

Lilly referred to the concept of a "realistic job preview." To this end, Hub made several culture videos using a montage of four locations in which employees shared a day in the life at the company. He said, "It's authentic because it features real people and shows the way they might be pulled in a bunch of different directions. It shows how there are lots of entrepreneurial opportunities which many people find exciting and a good cultural fit for them."

But does looking for a culture fit inevitably mean discrimination against candidates and a lack of diversity, as some observers claim? Not at all. Hiring for culture fit doesn't mean hiring people who are all the same. The values and attributes that make up an organizational culture can and should be reflected in a richly diverse workforce.

Most of your culture change will come by leading and inspiring the employees you already have, but there's a major advantage to keeping culture prominent throughout the interviewing, hiring, and orientation process. Companies should seek to hire diverse groups of people who also happen to align with the established values rather than trying to change a person's point of view after they've been brought on board. Here are some general questions you can ask to help determine a candidate's fit with your culture.

- Have you looked at our company values?
- Which ones most appeal to you and why?
- Describe your ideal work environment.
- Why do you want to work here?
- Tell me about a time when you worked for an organization and felt you were not a strong fit. Why was it a bad fit?
- Tell me about a time you felt you had to compromise your values to be successful at work. What made you feel that way and how did you handle it?

Here are some sample questions you might ask that should solicit specific, not theoretical, answers about specific values:

- Customer-centric: Tell me about a time you went the extra mile for a customer.
- Teamwork: Tell me about a time you had to collaborate closely with a difficult colleague. What was your approach? How did it turn out?
- Quality: Tell me about a time you found an error in your work. What did you do? How did you go about preventing it from happening again?
- Integrity: Sometimes we are asked to do things at work that we do not agree with. How have you handled it when this happened to you?

## Onboarding

According to outplacement consultants Challenger, Gray & Christmas, an estimated 25 percent of workers regret taking a new position within the first year. Millennials are reputed to have second thoughts within the first day or two and waste no time sharing their regrets all over social media.[26]

Onboarding is about much more than day one of an employee's employment. It encompasses several phases: the interview process, offer acceptance, the first day, and the next sixty to ninety days. The interview process includes how you, human resources, and your hiring managers treat candidates—because such treatment sets the stage for how people experience your culture. Getting back in touch with candidates in a timely manner, starting interviews promptly, making them feel comfortable during the interview process, and even the way you reject candidates all provide deep insight into your culture.

Once an offer is accepted, the next phase begins. Does your HR team allow paperwork to be completed prior to the first day of work? Most of it can be. Better yet, have you looked at technology that allows for much of this administrative processing to be done online? Use this time to let people know about the team they are joining. Provide names of coworkers. Have one or two key team members call the new hire to introduce themselves and welcome them. Send the newcomer a welcome package with a company hat or T-shirt. Share recent newsletters or a link to your intranet. About a week before they start, send them a detailed email giving them a heads-up on what their first few days will be like. Include a discussion of company values in your orientation and make sure that senior executives are available to meet and greet the newcomer.

People typically arrive on their first day with a case of the jitters, anxious to learn and understand how they fit in. They want to meet their coworkers and become familiar with their surroundings. So make sure that day one is more than sitting in an office filling out forms. As much as possible, set up phones, computers, and logins in advance, and have office supplies ready. Introductions, a tour, and a warm welcome go a long way. Allow for social time with team members. The hiring manager should take the new employee to lunch, ideally with a few colleagues.

An interesting onboarding approach is that taken by email marketing company Mailchimp. New employees don't actually do any work in their first week. Instead, they are showered with company swag, celebrated by their new coworkers, and introduced to representatives from each department to see how everything works together. Perhaps most pivotal to immersing new employees in this customer-first culture is when they join the research team for a "Customer Chat" to learn the needs and challenges of the customers and to get trained on the same Mailchimp app customers use. The internal motto is "Listen hard, change fast," and the new employee gains a good understanding of what this means during the onboarding process, particularly as it relates to the company culture of putting the customer first. Whether the person is working in marketing or accounting, they leave their first week with a strong understanding of what the company stands for and what their individual role is in helping the customer.[27]

Above all, look for ways throughout the first ninety days to immerse the new employee in your culture. And the sooner you start, the better. Within the first week, discuss their goals and the team goals, and continue those discussions regularly. Connect your new hire with a mentor who will guide him through your unwritten rules and help him appreciate your culture. If community service is an important part of your culture, involve him in an activity right away. Finally, talk about their role and its significance in the big picture.

An area most organizations neglect is the onboarding of new executives. According to Korn Ferry, about 40 percent of executives fail within the first eighteen months of taking up their new position. A major cause of this high failure rate is attributed to the executive not becoming acclimated to the corporate culture quickly enough.[28]

Other difficulties include a lack of clarity about the performance expected of them and their inability to build teamwork with staff and peers. Sound familiar? Yes, these are many of the same issues that employees at all levels face when they start a new job. Organizations assume executives know what they are doing and can figure things out, but executives need assistance assimilating into an organization's business and culture just as much as any new hire. Give extra attention to your executive onboarding to expedite their ability to make a strategic contribution and prevent derailment.

Hector Pena of Tailored Brands told me, "The core principle of any successful company is people working with people. When you have new leaders coming into an organization or being promoted, there has to be a system for getting them indoctrinated into your culture because every culture is unique."

Jennifer Speciale of McKinsey describes what happens if an onboarding process neglects to consider that people work best when they work collaboratively. "You can bring people in all day long, but if you're a bucket with a hole in it, it doesn't matter, they'll never last." And at McKinsey, they have an it-takes-a-village way of operating, so collaboration and mutual support are important.

In building teams all over the world, Speciale has closely observed the differences in the working styles of employees. "Some people want everything narrow and precise without a lot of wiggle room, a clear trajectory. Others are fine with wide-open spaces, riding with no handlebars. You don't have to hire in your own likeness to have a successful team you can grow and develop. You just have to be sensitive to what other people's needs are and how they define growth."

So how do you develop an effective onboarding process regardless of the employee's level? Here are some guidelines:

- Create a written plan.
- Establish accountability for the plan. Who will make sure it happens?

- Create ownership from the top, not just in HR, and have executive hands-on involvement.
- Build in opportunities for ongoing feedback from the participant so you can continue to improve the initiative.
- Assign a buddy or mentor to help support the new person.
- Schedule appropriate networking appointments for the newcomer.
- Early in the process (week one or two), provide workshops that guide the new employee through their onboarding plan and process. Provide them with tools with which they can customize the process to meet their needs. For example, give them a networking map so that they have a blueprint of who they need to meet and get to know. What teams should they job shadow?
- Create formal touchpoints and surveys every three months for the first year to get feedback on how the onboarding is progressing.

Now let's look at considerations when bringing executives onto the team. Here is a sample ninety-day plan for onboarding executives, broken down into thirty-day increments.

*First Thirty Days:*
- Understand cultural issues.
- Obtain consensus on top strategic priorities.
- Devise a ninety-day plan in writing.
- Get familiar with senior leadership relationships and determine potential risks and problem areas.
- Examine and consider improvements in the immediate organizational structure.

*Second Thirty Days:*

- Identify early wins.
- Identify learning priorities.
- Finalize an action plan to discuss with senior leaders.
- Refine specific job expectations and resource requirements with the executive's manager.

*Third Thirty Days:*

- Articulate a vision and engage the team.
- Develop and implement action plans to support execution of early wins.
- Strengthen alliances with key stakeholders.
- Maintain regular and effective communication processes with peers, superiors, and other stakeholders.

## Development

Richard Branson, the flamboyant founder and CEO of the Virgin Group, provides a thought-provoking perspective. "Train people well enough so they can leave, treat them well enough so they don't want to." He points out that many organizations resist investing in employee training and development because they fear that if they do so, people will leave, lured by competitors. He believes that this thinking is convoluted. "What they should fear is not training them and then they stay."

And training is a never-ending undertaking. As Xerox's Bala Sathyanarayanan told me, "Continuous management training is critical to employee development. Develop curriculum that enhances your managers' employee development and leadership skills."

Lack of development and the opportunity to learn are significant drivers of disengagement and turnover, especially with younger employees. You need to continually ask yourself how successful your organization is at growing your talent. A simple metric is the number of your managers that have been promoted from within. Ideally, you want to shoot for 70 to 80 percent, *assuming* you have the right raw talent and methods to develop their leadership skills in the first place.

One of my team members shared an experience from when she was the director of human resources for a mid-sized manufacturing firm. The company was making a huge culture shift from line manufacturing to lean manufacturing. Almost all of its frontline supervisors were homegrown. They had been great production employees and good leads. But none of them had worked in a lean manufacturing environment. This experience had to be hired from the outside.

Employees and leads were upset. They saw their career paths cut off and people from outside the industry supervising work teams. "But we really had no choice. We had to ramp up the knowledge and skills, and we had to do it fast." At the same time, they laid the foundation for future leaders. They developed and delivered training on lean concepts to all their employees and taught the incumbent supervisors and leads skills like root cause analysis, 5S, and other lean concepts. They also partnered with a local community college to improve the math and problem-solving skills of their workforce and cross-trained them. "We created a plan and process so that we could grow our talent internally again."

Many organizations, though, neglect the importance that learning and development plays at the top of the organization. Diane Leeming of AMITA Health told me about a program she helped deliver when she was with Kraft Foods. At that time, Kraft's cheese and dairy business unit was the lowest-performing unit globally. A new CEO was brought in to turn it around, and together, they focused on how they could invest in people to make the difference.

Their approach was to create a culture of accountability and high expectations. Every six months, they gathered together the top one hundred leaders, broke them into teams, and assigned tasks of solving key business problems. They were given four hours to strategize solutions. Kraft even staged a *Shark Tank* session featuring Mark Cuban and had the executives present to him.

The cheese and dairy business unit was very proud of the fact that they'd won an industry gold award for the best cheddar. But Mark Cuban issued a reality check. "Show your award on ESPN, because your consumers don't care." The message was clear. You cannot rest on your laurels and you had better know what is really important to the people who buy your product.

Kraft also brought in outside training and did a three-day deep dive, seeking solutions to their business challenges. The result: In sixteen quarters, they experienced double-digit top and bottom-line growth. Explained Leeming, "If you are intentional in what you expect from your business and intentional about the culture you need, you can turn your business around."

Diane Leeming joined AMITA Health after a long, successful career with Kraft Foods. While she had found Kraft to be a great company, she reevaluated her work role when her mother passed away after an extended journey with Alzheimer's. Between grief and a lot of questioning about why she was really put on Earth, she had difficulty getting out of bed in the morning. She did some serious soul-searching and took a leap of faith, landing at AMITA Health, a large faith-based hospital system in Illinois. Says Leeming, "It's all about the patient and their families. The reason all of our employees get out of bed every day, whether they're nurses or office workers, is to help the patient. We hire people who fit the culture of compassion and caregiving."

Leeming's life changed. Her goals changed. She delivered development programs at Kraft, but she was also a recipient of company development. Yes, when you develop your staff, they may leave. Some will leave anyway. When they stay, the company and its customers benefit. When they leave, their former employer's reputation is enhanced by the expertise they bring with them to the new company. It ends up being win-win.

## Performance Management and Coaching

Performance management can be a primary driver of organizational effectiveness, but it rarely is. According to a Towers Watson survey, only 30 percent of employees say their organization's performance management process improves performance. When was the last time you polled your employees on the value of your process?[29]

There are at least a couple of flaws in most organizations' performance management systems. One of the biggest is the emphasis on the form itself. Emphasis on the process rather than the true purpose, which is to improve performance, is a second flaw.

Think about NASA's Project Apollo. The outcome they sought was to land a man on the moon and bring him back safely to Earth. They did not know how they were going to pull off this astounding feat. Half the technology they needed had not yet been invented. But the team of scientists and engineers coalesced around their collective knowledge to make the mission a success. And the technology developed on behalf of that project took computer hardware and software, robotics, and many other industries forward in ways that would not have happened so quickly had it not been for Apollo—right down to the laptop you probably use on a regular basis. If they had been working according to a traditional performance management system, the course of history would probably have changed.

Traditional performance management is ineffective for two key reasons. The first is that goals are set annually, but the work environment and the market can change daily. The process has no built-in agility to compensate for the rapid change organizations face. Second, people need ongoing and continuous feedback to improve. Once a year will not cut it. Could you imagine the result if a football coach only gave his players feedback once a year?

Deconic, the recently formed jewelry division of Brooks Brothers, is also rolling out a new performance management system. Matteo Del Vecchio, CEO of this division, is leading a significant merger and re-branding of Deconic, Carolee, and Alexis Bittar. He emphasized the importance of having the executive team lead the charge to implement the performance management strategy. "The process will start with the leadership team. They need to try it on their own skin first before we introduce it company-wide. They need to own the process and fully understand it."

Performance management is all about providing direction, feedback, and recognition. It is not about forms, ratings, and rankings. Above all, it is not an administrative process. It is a leadership, coaching, and communication tool. High performance cultures understand that expectations, and especially expectations around outcomes, need to be clear and frequently discussed. Feedback needs to be ongoing, not once a year. Leaders need to be great coaches who focus primarily on employees' strengths.

A study by the Human Capital Institute reinforces this point. It found, "A strong coaching culture is correlated with higher employee engagement and stronger financial performance." In the study, 62 percent of employees of organizations with strong coaching cultures rated themselves as "highly engaged," and 51 percent of companies with strong coaching cultures reported above average revenue growth in comparison to peer groups.[30]

Coaching means working with employees in a thought provoking and motivational way to maximize their personal and professional potential. It is a critical component to create performance improvement, building and strengthening your culture, and forging deep employee engagement.

Significantly, coaching is a learnable skill. It requires training, and it should be built into your leadership and management development strategies. Coaching skills center around asking questions, listening, and helping team members apply their strengths on the job. Your goal is to help employees transition from being managers who direct the work of others to leaders who engage, inspire, and empower employees.

How can you build a coaching-based performance culture in your organization? You can begin by posing this question to your executive team: What kind of culture does our organization need for us to thrive over the next ten years? A frank discussion about this question will help you develop a road map to your desired culture. Coaching is the single most powerful tool you and your leaders can use to bring your people along this path.

## People Making It Happen at UniFirst

The core values at UniFirst Corporation, a $1.59 billion uniform rental company, typify those of so many culture-minded companies: customer focus, commitment to quality, transparency, teamwork, and respect for others. In 2017, UniFirst won two Bronze Stevie Awards in the Sales Training or Coaching Program of the Year category at the eleventh annual Stevie Awards for Sales and Customer Service—the world's top honors for customer service, contact center, business development, and sales professionals. They also won similar awards in 2017 and 2016 and have been rated as a Best Company to Sell For.[31]

"Our values are not just a poster on the wall," declares National Sales Manager Steve Chikerotis. "Even though we're publicly traded, the founding family is very much in control of the business, so a commitment to equality and respect for others holds true throughout the organization. Our culture is really led by example from the top down." To make sure the corporate culture is understood, UniFirst has a Care Team that flies into major hubs throughout North America and spends several days interviewing people in different departments to get their perception of the company.

That culture spreads throughout the workforce of more than twelve thousand in over 230 facilities in North America and Europe, including customer service centers, nuclear decontamination facilities, cleanroom locations, distribution centers, and manufacturing plants. Says Chikerotis, "Since I can't make three hundred thousand customers happy on my own, I believe that if customers come first, employees come before them."

In his fifteen-year career at UniFirst, Chikerotis has managed sales teams at local, regional, and national levels, with historically low turnover rates at each level. His team tracks their success on a custom dashboard that highlights each individual's goals and accomplishments and, as Chikerotis puts it, "We celebrate the living daylights out of every win, big or small."

As National Sales Manager, Chikerotis turned a lone wolf environment into a team environment. He focuses on modeling, coaching, and mentoring to get people to the success levels they wish to achieve—and that is not limited to professional goals. "I put an immense amount of effort into trying to tie in their professional goals to their personal goals and tracking to make sure they're on pace for what they want, as opposed to what I want."

Chikerotis said that at UniFirst, there's a team dynamic with ongoing training and a culture of continuous improvement and the sharing of best practices. For instance, Chikerotis created a shared drive, a corporate server to which everyone has access, which initially just contained posts from his tenure as corporate accounts manager—presentations, cost analysis, creative prospecting ideas, and so on. Once he shared with others the "secrets" that work, the folders slowly started to build as others participated. They began using each other as resources, not just him. The team took ownership of the culture and became engaged, not just as individuals in it for themselves, but as a team. "At this point, if someone comes up with a good idea, they almost rush to put it on the drive to show the team, whereas it used to be every person for him or herself—an 'if you don't catch any food, you don't eat that night' mindset."

It took the company's lead sales rep the longest to get on board because he had enjoyed more than a decade of success doing his own thing. "But once he saw the benefit of everyone working together towards larger overall sales, he became one of our biggest contributors to the teaching process."

Chikerotis' team meetings are a sounding board for everyone. He asks the group what they need to stop doing and what they need to start doing. These answers then feed into course corrections they make on a monthly basis.

The bottom line, says Chikerotis, is that it's not what you say, it's what you do. "We are a very transparent organization, internally and externally to our customers and prospects. We pride ourselves on being the most transparent company in the industry and sharing data that customers and prospects aren't accustomed to receiving from our competitors—and that helps tremendously."

———

There are no great companies without great people. Sourcing, hiring, onboarding, and developing your people are critical. After all, they are your most expensive and most valuable asset. But if you truly want to know what impact this investment is making, you need to develop ways to *measure* this impact. And while it may seem impossible to measure something that seems as "soft" as culture, it is not only not impossible, it's critical to do so. Let's delve into how to do that.

# Measure

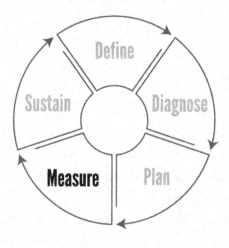

*KPIs are real-time indicators of how your initiatives are succeeding. You will fail 100% of the time if you are don't measure what you are doing.*
–Andrew Koehler, Human Capital Management Consultant, ADP

For a long time, culture has been considered a "soft topic" and too subjective to measure. Yet, without measurement, there is no way to determine if you are making progress or if you need to change course.

The first thing to bear in mind is that no two company cultures are alike. Sure, they may share things in common such as similar values, but how those values are lived, reinforced, and aligned with business strategy will be unique to each organization. This means that common metrics, such as benchmarks, may not be very helpful. This also means that whatever you decide to measure needs to be clearly linked to *your* business purpose, core strategies, and goals. A guiding principle comes from Zappos CEO Tony Hsieh's book, *Delivering Happiness*, in which he emphasizes the importance of profits, passion, and purpose. All three should be measured.

## Using Culture Surveys as a Measurement Tool

Another important consideration is how consistent your culture is from multiple perspectives, including levels of employees, business units, and geographies. You will need to figure out ways to measure the alignment between culture and behavior from all these angles. The culture surveys discussed earlier are a great place to start. In other words, first diagnose your culture, then plan your strategy for changing it over time, and finally, plan how you are going to track your progress. Too many organizations either skip this last step or make it too complicated to sustain.

Dr. Tobias Witte, a business intelligence executive and President of WITTBIX with many years of expertise helping organizations measure results, recommends treating culture change and related communication with employees similarly to how customer-centric organizations treat customers. Such organizations survey customers regularly with simple surveys: Would you recommend us to others? Would you use this service again? How would you rate the product you recently purchased from us? Companies also closely monitor and measure customer website traffic, including things like which areas of the website they visit and the length of time spent on the website, both as a whole and on individual areas. The same techniques can be used to track employee visits to your company intranet, especially if the intranet is being used to share important information about culture change or company values.

In this fast-paced world constantly buffeted by change, you want to develop measurements that are frequent, quick, and ongoing. Don't make your engagement or culture surveys a complex project. Instead, looks for ways to build measures into a regular routine. After all, you don't measure your sales once a year or every other year. You need to embed culture measurements into the way you run your business as a whole.

Think about culture change the way you think about any business initiative, because that is exactly what it is. Surveys do not need to be complicated or lengthy. Your employees will be more likely to respond if they can do so quickly and with ease. The surveys do need to be frequent enough to track progress, especially in times of rapid change. Asking them to fill out surveys quarterly will not tax people or create survey fatigue. Just be sure to share survey results and provide regular updates on how you are responding to them.

## Asking the Right Questions Matters

When companies merge, they often have disparate cultures. Employees are nervous, and companies risk a rapid drop in engagement—if not the flight of some employees. Dr. Tobias Witte shared a personal experience from early in his career.

He was working in Germany for a very large IT services organization that had just been acquired by a similar company based elsewhere in Europe. The C-Suite realized the merger was impacting all levels of operations, creating a hectic and stressful work environment. The senior executives wanted to get a better feeling for what was happening at all levels of employees. "They wisely realized how employees were feeling was not particularly transparent, whether in regard to changes in their corporate values or changes in basic processes, such as submission of travel expenses."

To address these concerns, the company established an ongoing series of focus groups. They invited employees at all levels to frankly discuss current challenges. They asked a lot of open-ended questions. Among them were the following: How are you feeling about the latest changes in our values? Do you feel included in these discussions? Do you understand the new values?

They also asked more targeted questions about system and policy changes, recognizing these sorts of changes, although common with mergers and acquisitions, also create anxiety and stress. An interesting example was the new travel and expense policy and system. Under normal circumstances, such policies are commonplace, and even when not perfect, they are not much more than an annoyance. But this leadership team realized that such changes could be problematic for employees already overwhelmed with change. In other words, they carefully and purposefully focused on a variety of employee pain points. In the focus groups, they asked employees how they felt about such policies and if the system changes were working.

They even went a step further and asked employees if they wanted to volunteer to participate in change groups to help develop new processes, enhance changes that were taking place, and be part of the solution. This was well received by many employees. Said Dr. Witte, "I was highly motivated to participate and help improve and speed up the culture change process. In fact, this was a key factor in motivating me to stay on with the company."

The information gathered in the focus groups was supplemented with frequent employee surveys, first bi-weekly, and then on a monthly basis after about six months. They asked questions in the survey about how employees were feeling, using a one-to-ten rating scale. This made it easy to establish a baseline and track improvements and gaps that in turn could be dived into more deeply in subsequent focus groups.

Dr. Witte compared this process to that which many customer-centric companies follow with their customers. Such surveys can be as simple as asking people how satisfied they are about a certain service, and the same can be easily asked of employees. Employees respond positively to being asked for their opinions and ideas, as long as they see response and action based on their input.

The Culture Journey Game Plan below will help you lay out your strategy. Remember, tracking culture change is just one part of your planning and measurement process. Your goal is to see positive culture change trends over time that correlate with positive business metrics or KPI changes throughout your journey. A sample scorecard to track progress follows the game plan. I have also provided you with a sample completed game plan for steps one through six (the additional steps will be very specific to your organization, making a sample difficult to provide) and a sample completed scorecard. In both the Culture Journey Game Plan and Scorecard examples, I have selected business imperatives and metrics relevant to the sample company, a specialty retail organization.

## Culture Journey Game Plan

1. Purpose: Why does your organization exist?
2. Top three business imperatives. (Below are typical ones.)
   - Revenue growth
   - Market share
   - Profitability
   - Customer retention
   - Time to market
   - Quality
   - Customer satisfaction
   - Productivity
   - Other
3. Select three corporate values you want to focus on. Choose values that will be particularly impactful in driving your top three business imperatives.

4. Use business data to identify the strengths and weaknesses of the top three business imperatives you selected.

5. Use data and information from employee surveys, focus groups, and your observation tools.

6. Develop tactics to address each of the business imperative strengths and weaknesses and each of the values you identified. After developing the tactics to address your strengths and weaknesses, try to anticipate and identify potential barriers to their execution. Document approaches to overcoming these barriers should they occur.

7. Develop a communication plan for sharing your plan throughout your entire organization.

8. Goal Setting: Each relevant work group develops 3-5 goals for each of the business tactics. Relevant work groups will vary depending on your organization. Examples might be departments, business units, geographic regions, or a combination of these. Goals need to be focused on measurable outcomes, such as KPIs, cost reduction, percent increases, etc.

9. Develop rewards and recognition strategies for the goals identified.

10. Clarify the key metrics you will track and report on.

11. Develop celebration strategies and activities as milestones are met.

12. Develop interventions for goals and initiatives that are not moving forward or being achieved as quickly as is needed.

## Sample Plan for Steps 1-6 for XYZ Women's Boutique

1. Purpose: Why does your organization exist?
   *To make fashionable, professional apparel affordable to working women.*

2. Top three business imperatives
   - *Revenue growth*
   - *Profitability*
   - *Customer satisfaction*

3. Three corporate values to focus on
   - *Customer-centric*
   - *Teamwork*
   - *Positive Work Environment*

4. Business imperatives: strengths and weaknesses
   Strengths:
   - *Revenue Growth: Up 12 percent against goal of 10 percent*
   - *Customer satisfaction: Net Promoter Score 9.2; average customer spend up 2 percent over LY*

   Weaknesses:
   - *Profitability: 27 percent vs. LY 32 percent and goal of 35 percent*

5. Values: Strengths and Weaknesses
   Strengths:
   - *Customer-centric: Rated 4.5 out of 5 by employees on values survey*

   Weaknesses:
   - *Teamwork: Feedback from focus groups not consistent. Varies significantly from department to department. Employee Values Survey rating 3.2.*

- *Positive Work Environment: Engagement Survey work environment rating 3.0; lowest scored category. Turnover of high performers at 33 percent.*

6. Business Imperatives and Values Tactics

| Business Imperatives | Tactics | Potential Barriers | Overcome Barriers |
|---|---|---|---|
| **Weaknesses:** Teamwork | - Do deep dive into focus group and values survey data to determine where teamwork is weaker. <br> - Set up managers' meetings to discuss and develop action plans with HR. <br> - Review exit interview information for further data. <br> - Determine if management training is needed on how to lead and develop teams. | Some managers may not be very adept at building teamwork | Assign a coach or mentor to help them |
| Positive Work Environment | - Do segmented analysis of engagement scores in this category. Where are the lowest scoring departments and regions? | | |
| | -Train managers on how to develop and implement action plans to improve. <br> - Review comments from employees on this topic to look for patterns. <br> - Work with employee committees to develop improvement plans. | Managers do not follow through on plans | VPs hold them accountable; build into goals and formal expectations for Performance Reviews |

# Scorecard

The purpose of the scorecard is to help you create a simple, visual tracking and reporting tool to measure progress on an ongoing basis. What you call certain sections will depend on your organization and what you currently measure as well as the business drivers for your industry. The key to making this process work is consistent monitoring of progress as often as is needed. In the example I provide, the tracking is quarterly. There may be metrics you need to track more frequently (monthly, for example), and you simply adapt this template accordingly. You may also need to add or delete key metrics depending on what your organization tracks.

In addition, let your normal reporting approach determine how you report results. Some organizations prefer to report actual numbers, while others prefer a green-yellow-red color coding for their scorecard.

### Culture and Business Imperative Scorecard

| | SOURCE | CURRENT STATE | DESIRED STATE | Q1 | Q2 | Q3 | Q4 |
|---|---|---|---|---|---|---|---|
| **CULTURE/ VALUES** | Engagement scores | | | | | | |
| | Pulse survey score | | | | | | |
| | Undesirable turnover* | | | | | | |
| | Focus group feedback | | | | | | |
| | Unique visits to company intranet where new values are posted | | | | | | |
| **BUSINESS METRICS**** | Sales/Revenue Growth | | | | | | |
| | Net profit | | | | | | |
| | Sales per employee | | | | | | |
| | Customer satisfaction | | | | | | |

| | SOURCE | CURRENT STATE | DESIRED STATE | Q1 | Q2 | Q3 | Q4 |
|---|---|---|---|---|---|---|---|
| **BUSINESS METRICS**\*\* | Stock price | | | | | | |
| | Market share | | | | | | |
| **KPIs** | Quality scores | | | | | | |
| | Complete shipment scores | | | | | | |
| | Inventory turnover | | | | | | |
| **CULTURE/ VALUES** | Engagement scores | 80% | 90% | | | | |
| | Undesirable turnover\* | 33% | 20% | | | | |
| | Unique visits to company intranet where new values are posted | 68% | 75% | | | | |
| **BUSINESS METRICS** | Revenue Growth | 10% over LY | 12% | | | | |
| | Net profit | 35% | 27% | | | | |
| | Sales per employee | 100K | 120K | | | | |
| | Net Promoter Score | 9.2 | 9.4 | | | | |
| **KPIs** | Complete shipment scores | 97.5% | 98% | | | | |
| | Inventory turnover | 8 | 8 | | | | |

\* Undesirable turnover is defined as turnover of employees you do not want to lose. These can include top performers, high potentials, and/or hard to fill critical positions.

\*\* The business metrics and KPIs you track will vary depending on what you identify in your Culture Journey Game Plan. What I have included here are the most common ones.

## Culture Is Not a Soft Topic, and It Can Be Measured

In addition to surveys and scorecards, it is important for CEOs to stay actively involved in the culture change process. Most leaders have regular one-on-one meetings with their direct reports. Make sure to include discussion around culture, the behaviors expected to model company values, and the progress each direct report is making with their own teams.

Culture is not a *soft topic*. In fact, changing an organization's culture is quite *hard*. Establishing a baseline with a thorough diagnosis, developing clear plans, and holding people accountable to their commitments take time and effort. If you do not measure your progress along the way, your efforts will not get you the business results you desire.

# Sustaining the Change

*The real return on culture happened when we started getting
more deliberate about it. By writing it down. By debating it.
By taking it apart, polishing the pieces and putting it
back together. Iterating. Again. And again.*
–Dharmesh Shah, Cofounder, HubSpot

More than 70 percent of change initiatives fail to meet stakeholder expectations, according to a 2000 article in the *Harvard Business Review*.[32] As shocking as this statistic might sound, it is not a new concern. In 1849, French journalist Jean-Baptise Alphonse Karr wrote what was to become a famous epigram: "Plus ça change, plus c'est la même chose." Or if you prefer English, "The more things change, the more they stay the same."

More recently, a 2013 study by global professional services firm Towers Watson revealed that 55 percent of employers feel their change management initiatives meet their initial objectives. While that is also not an encouraging statistic, what's worse is that only 25 percent said they were able to keep the momentum going for the long haul. The survey blamed the lack of continued success partly on companies' "inability to prepare and train managers to be effective change leaders."[33]

Revitalizing or changing your culture is a daunting task, and failure is expensive. Many changes get stuck at the implementation phase. Others flounder when strategies and initiatives meet resistance from employees, who often succumb to old habits. Sustaining culture change is particularly challenging because we ask people to alter deeply ingrained and sometimes unconscious behaviors and habits.

## Why Culture Change Initiatives Fail

Let's assume you're convinced that culture matters and that you and your leadership team have an essential role to play in transforming your organization. Such understanding is a great start, but taken alone, it is not enough to keep you safe from failure. The efforts you make in defining your new or revitalized culture, identifying and communicating your values, diagnosing your gaps, and designing well-thought-out plans will be for naught if you do not also have a strategy to sustain your direction for the long term.

First, consider the top reasons why culture change initiatives fail. Talk about these with both your leadership team and rank-and-file employees so you can work together to prevent them from happening.

### *Lack of Executive Commitment*

Leaders are supposed to lead. If you're not fully embracing a change in culture, why should anyone else? Culture change is a strategic and true competitive advantage, but many company leaders just don't get it and don't take it seriously enough.

"You have to identify what culture truly means and then make sure that it happens," says Matt Hawksley, a regional director for global logistics company BDP International. "It's a byproduct of leadership that should cascade down throughout the organization."

It's crucial to understand that the corporate DNA is comprised of a cross-section of departments, regions, and up-and-coming leaders that truly embody what you want the culture to be, he says. Ultimately, he emphasizes, it's up to you, the leader. "Someone else is not going to do it for you. When it comes to culture and leadership, it has to start today, and it starts with you."

I'd take this insight a step further. It not only has to start with you, it has to be sustained by you.

### Don't Make It Only a Human Resources Initiative

Don't think of culture as something that's the exclusive domain of your HR department. I have made this point before, but it is so important, it's worth reemphasizing. This is the corollary to the failure reason above. You want human resources actively involved in strategy development and implementation, but they should not lead the charge. That's because culture change is a business strategy, not just a people strategy

### Lack of Middle Management Buy-In

So HR is an important contributor, but who should also be actively involved in the development and maintenance of culture? Middle management, for sure. Middle management has a very strong influence on culture because they have the most immediate connection to most of your employees—and often customers, as well. Middle managers are instrumental in creating a deep personal commitment to change. They truly influence the emotional a-ha moments, the vital lightbulb moments that need to occur to create momentum.

### *Insufficient Ongoing Communication and Reinforcement*

Leaders face a lot of problems, but poor communication is one they create for themselves. When you keep your messaging locked up in your ivory tower, you're only imprisoning your culture. You have to be open and transparent—today more than ever.

Jonathan Evans of thyssenkrupp North America emphasizes that transparency may be an overused word in communications, but that doesn't detract from its significance. "Be open and honest. Walk the talk. And be accountable. In any organization, there's always resistance to change. One of the key things we have to do is manage that change process, manage expectations about where we're going and how we can get there. You don't want to over-promise and under-deliver."

Communication is also a constant and ongoing process, not simply something you do at a quarterly meeting. With regular communication, you have an intimate pulse of your team and the issues at hand. And that can mean casual conversation around the water cooler, says Dan Calista, founder and CEO of Vynamic. Formal communication has its place as well. Calista holds a virtual thirty-minute meeting with his team members every two weeks. It's called TACT Time Tuesday, which stands for transparency, awareness, clarity, and trust—all elements we have discussed.

## Supporting Growth over Six Decades by Emphasizing Culture

Before we look at best practices, let's take a look at a company that has grown and evolved over six decades and across continents, thanks, in part, to maintaining a good culture.

When Baker McKenzie opened its doors in 1949, it boasted four lawyers, a secretary, and fees of just $75,000. Today, it's the second largest law firm in the world with 4,700 attorneys and revenue of $2.67 billion.

Steadily, the firm has expanded into seventy-seven offices across forty-seven countries. Growth like that, across countries and continents, presents challenges in terms of maintaining a strong corporate culture. How has Baker McKenzie pulled it off?

"Our growth has been organic, giving us a strong, common culture that runs through our firm," they say. "For six decades, we have followed clients into new markets, each time establishing offices driven by local lawyers and talent."

But overall, it's teamwork that holds the firm together. "Baker McKenzie was formed with collegiality. It's in our DNA. It's the way we have always operated," Global Human Resources Director Alan Tecktiel told me. "Each office is independent but requires a high level of collegiality and collaboration. It's not a cutthroat dog-eat-dog kind of environment. It's a place where people really like to work together to, first and foremost, help the client. It's a culture of friendship, while at the same time, maintaining performance and holding people accountable."

Teamwork extends to making everyone at every level in every country feel connected.

Adds Tecktiel, "We're working on making everyone feel part of a global family. We want the person in a small, remote office to realize that he or she is part of a global team, working together to make sure our technology tools are functioning properly and securely."

Baker McKenzie's North America Professional Development Director Ann Hopkins Avery agrees that there's a great need for inclusion when running a worldwide enterprise. "Baker McKenzie is one of the most progressive law firms I've encountered. It is unique in that the company started with a global objective and has always been inclusive of differences. That's an essential ingredient when building a culture for such a large international organization." Equality, humanity, and tolerance are all a part of that inclusiveness and what Hopkins Avery refers to as being a good citizen at Baker McKenzie.

Establishing a winning culture, according to the Baker McKenzie executives, requires leadership from the top, transparency, innovation, and flexibility. They believe that cultural change requires leadership support and a broad view of project impact. Projects are viewed from the standpoint of impact to the organization as a whole, not just team impact.

"Transparency of communication is a big part ... basically opening up the veil to say: Here's what's happening in the executive committee meeting, here are the projects we're working on, here's a refreshed vision," says Tecktiel. "It's letting everyone know what the organization is going to look like and how they can be part of it, building up excitement."

And while it's important to lead by example, you need to be careful what message you transmit to your team. Hopkins Avery told me that to get caught up on projects, she got into the habit of sending out emails at ten o'clock at night until she realized the message that sent. "I didn't want my team to think I was creating a culture where I expected them to respond late at night. Now I'm more mindful of that. So if I write emails at night, I schedule them to go out in regular business hours."

Tecktiel and Hopkins Avery both stress the need for innovation. That extends to how they do business and how Baker McKenzie treats employees.

"There is nothing about the way we've done business in the past that is a given in the future—other than the importance of focusing on the client. In any organization, a lot of employees remember some golden era of how things used to be, so it's not easy for any of us to think freshly about something," says Tecktiel.

And Hopkins Avery points out that to attract and retain top talent, you must be innovative. "We're in a different world compared to twenty years ago. We have a lot of dual working parents; we have a lot of people caring for aging parents. We have to be innovative about how people do their work, where they work, and when they work."

In response to an internal engagement survey in 2017, Baker McKenzie rolled out a program called bAgile. It's a flexible work initiative that includes working remotely, alternative hours, part-time work, and time out—taking unpaid breaks for personal reasons. The bAgile program helps to support work-life balance. Says Hopkins Avery, "Baker does a very good job of focusing on the whole person. You bring your whole self to a job, and Baker acknowledges and provides support for balancing employees' personal and professional demands."

Management may be willing to make certain changes on a temporary basis, she says, and in doing so, they achieve a few small wins and build trust and relationships in the process.

## Best Practices to Drive Continued Success

Now that we've delved into potential reasons for failure, let's consider what you can do to ensure success. Let's look at a number of practical strategies and tactics to sustain the culture changes you and your team have worked so hard to create. Leading by example is a bit of a cliché, but a wise practice, nonetheless. So how do you turn "lead by example" into practical actions? Here are some best practices I have gleaned from executives I have interviewed and from many years of client interaction.

### Let Purpose and Values Take Center Stage

Amber Hurdle, author of *The Bombshell Business Woman*, says that values are the measuring stick for how you make business decisions.[34] Purpose and values are the centerpiece of any corporate culture. You and your leadership team not only have to live them, you must make sure everyone else knows what they are. Broadcast them using every means at your disposal. Here are some specific examples of what you should do:

- Talk about your purpose and values often. When communicating strategic decisions or new direction, share how they support and reinforce your purpose and values. Values are certainly words to live by, and they are also a powerful tool for reinforcing the culture you want to sustain.

- Enlist your marketing team to create some graphics that represent your values. Kick off every face-to-face and online meeting or presentation with these graphics. Images are processed by the brain faster and easier than words. Use graphics to your advantage.

- Provide talking points for managers so they can discuss a different value at every meeting.

- Hold people accountable for living the values by instituting multiple feedback loops on how well employees demonstrate organizational values. These could include things like performance management processes, recognition strategies, and policy revisions.

- Revisit and refresh your values. Make sure they continue to serve your culture and people over time. "We reinvent ourselves consistently and constantly in order to make sure that our culture is aligned with the marketplace and what our clients are looking for," says Shaun Rudy, a senior vice president with a large media agency. "We're always asking ourselves, what can we do differently to elevate the work we do for our clients and their business?" The team, he says, regard themselves as innovation warriors, always thinking about how they can be a little bit more on the cutting edge.

### Communicate, Communicate, Communicate

Communication should be easy. It should be second nature for corporate executives. After all, we all communicate one way or another in our everyday lives. Unless you're at a vending machine, you can't even buy a cup of coffee without communicating. But in business, company leaders sometimes act as if their employees should be mind readers or communicate without expressing their expectations with any degree of clarity or forthrightness.

Charles Lilly of Hub International holds regular best practice calls for effective team communication and to ensure the organization continues to learn and adapt to changing circumstances. "They're all pretty candid conversations. We don't sugarcoat stuff. We're changing rapidly, so people need to understand that what they did last year might not work this year. They can't just regurgitate the same process."

Andrea Belmont at Nielsen agrees. "We all need to be connected and not afraid to open up and say what's on our minds." Executives at all levels need to be approachable and available to members of the team. "Every leader at Nielsen is open and honest and willing to talk to you."

### Keep Values in Mind When You Hire

There will come a time when a hiring manager in your organization tries to pressure you, their manager, or the human resources team to bring someone with great skills on board even if they are not a solid fit from a values perspective. Maybe the person is a killer sales rep for the competition or a hotshot thought leader in your field. Chances are high, though, that if they're not a good match to your culture and values, they will not last. They are likely to frustrate coworkers and be unhappy themselves. As discussed earlier, the cost of a poor hire is significant. Why position both your organization and the person you hire for failure?

### Don't Let Poor Hiring Decisions Fester

Anyone who has done a certain amount of hiring has at some point made a hiring mistake. It happens. Take a lesson from Tony Hsieh, the CEO of Zappos, who told Forbes in a 2010 interview, "We're willing to give up short-term profits or revenue growth to make sure we have the best culture. In fact, after orientation we offer people $2,000 not to work at Zappos. The ones who stay are right for our culture."

Warren Buffet has been quoted as saying that one should look for integrity, intelligence, and energy when hiring, but that if you don't have integrity, the other two qualities will kill you. This is good counsel from one of the most successful businessmen in the world, but if you do manage to hire someone who does not possess one of your values—like integrity—don't compound the problem by keeping them on.

This does not mean you have carte blanche to capriciously fire or treat people disrespectfully. Just because someone is not a good fit at your organization doesn't mean they won't be a great asset elsewhere. But if an individual is not going to be able to work and live the values you have determined are best for your business, they are not going to be happy. In fact, they are likely already unhappy and thinking they made a bad decision in joining you. A kind but frank discussion can help resolve many such issues. If given the opportunity to move on while saving face, many people will take it.

### Incorporate Values into Your Sales and Service Processes

Your sales and service teams come face-to-face with your customers more than other employees. In particular, you want them to deeply understand and buy in to your culture and values because the customers will see through them if they don't.

Constantly evaluate your processes to make sure they're in alignment with the customer. Every time you work on a new process or change a current one, ask if the change is going to serve the customer.

Evaluate all processes at least yearly from the points of view of your customer, your culture, and your values.

## Train Your Managers on How to Sustain Your Culture

Continuous management training is critical to all employee development. "Engaging the hearts, minds, and hands of talent is the most sustainable source of competitive advantage," says Greg Harris, President and CEO of Quantum Workplace. Harris highly encourages the use of assessment tools such as 360° feedback that allow managers to hear from their teams on how well *they* are doing to ensure that development is a two-way street.

In addition, managers themselves should be mentored to become better leaders. Xerox's Bala Sathyanarayanan says, "Most times, organizations tend to emphasize mentoring newer and younger employees, but mentorship can also change the game for your management-level employees."

## Train Your Field Employees

How should you structure training and culture reinforcement for frontline and field employees? Steve Gonzalez of KONE points out that these employees are the face of the organization, and to succeed, they need support. He provides an example of what that kind of support can look like. The company assembles stakeholders who agree on universal success factors, such as zero accidents, zero defects, and a delighted customer. Then, in partnership with the customer, they define what delighted actually means. "They are the most important stakeholder, so engaging them is critical."

As new team members join, communication of these tenets is core to onboarding. KONE also uses the same universal success factors when making decisions. Does it improve safety, deliver quality, and improve the result? "In this way, we constantly reinforce them as basic tenets, creating a culture centered around common goals," says

Gonzalez. "While field employees are most often seen as the 'face' of the organization, their success depends on outstanding support that's sometimes far away from direct customer contact."

### Involve Employees at All Levels in Reinforcing Your Culture

You need to achieve actual buy-in throughout your entire organization: top-down, bottom-up, and everything in between. One weak link can uncouple all of your best efforts. Culture committees are a powerful way to involve many levels of employees, as well as multiple locations, to build your culture in an organic manner and ensure that it's shared across regions and sustained as you grow.

Southwest Airlines has had culture committees in place since 1990. Southwest CEO Gary Kelly and Chairman Emeritus Herb Kelleher have often said that it is probably the company's most important committee. Culture services teams are responsible for recognition, appreciation, and celebration of Southwest's more than fifty thousand employees.

### Identify a Chief Culture Officer

I have discussed and stressed at considerable length the importance of culture being led by the C-Suite. While grassroots participation is pivotal to develop and sustain your culture, the vision and accountability need to come from the top.

An increasing number of companies have recognized this new dynamic and added to the C-Suite the position of Chief Culture Officer (CCO), sometimes also called Chief Transformation Officer. Another possible title might be Chief Talent Officer. Such roles might reside in human resources, and I have seen examples where the Chief Human Resources Officer is co-titled Chief Culture Officer. Alternatively, the Chief Culture Officer can report direct to the CEO as a role of its own.

The CCO's role is to promote communication, alignment, goals, and recognition to support and sustain an organization's culture. The trend is for startups to institute this position early in their development to build a culture that reflects the values and morals of the founders—before a contrary culture emerges by default. Large and enterprise-level companies more commonly hire a CCO during periods of rapid growth or decline, after a merger or acquisition, or to support a change in overall strategy.

According to *Fortune Magazine*, the best-known example of the latter approach is Google, which added Chief Culture Officer to the job title of the head of HR, Stacy Sullivan, in 2006. One of her responsibilities was to protect key elements of Google's scrappy, open-source cultural core as the company evolved into a gargantuan, world-dominant multinational.[35]

More traditional companies, even in the financial industry, have hired culture chiefs as well. One example is North Jersey Community Bank, which recently appointed Maria Gendelman as its Chief Culture Officer. CEO Frank Sorrentino says that he encountered resistance from his board when he argued for the position because the job description was a little tough to define and something the traditionalists struggled to embrace. But having that position for the bank was a differentiator, and Gendelman sees no reason why it shouldn't become status quo in the industry. "Could every bank utilize a protector of the culture as part of the team?" she asks. Answering her own question, she adds, "Absolutely."

A chief culture officer can help make sure your evolving strategies, ideas, and implementations generated at all levels of the organization are in sync with your overall mission and business imperatives.

### Create Traditions

Every culture in the world has its own set of traditions, and the business environment should be no different. "People cannot derive purpose and meaning from work if they are not comfortable," says Stephen Hart of the Federal Reserve Bank of Philadelphia.

Traditions can include rituals, fun celebrations, and stories—all dynamic ways to create the comfort to which Steve Hart refers.

When you develop such traditions, you drive company culture on the emotional level. You strengthen esprit de corps, the ability to maintain group loyalty and cohesiveness in good times and bad. The great thing about many of these rituals is that they don't have to be elaborate or expensive to have lasting impact.

Don't wait for perfection—or you are going to wait a long time. And don't ignore what you're already doing right. Somewhere inside the processes and strategies that need attention, there are working pieces that should be acknowledged and celebrated. Perhaps it's a certain division or a new policy that's making a positive impact on customer satisfaction. Whatever it is, big or small, highlight it to show that you do see the positives amongst the negatives. As Marcia Lyssy, Chief Human Resources Officer at BDP International, put it, "When you're trying to move mountains, it's important to acknowledge what is successful and reinforce the positives."

Celebrations are an impactful tradition and can be as simple or as complicated as you want to make them. One of my favorites is The Home Depot's "Orange you glad it's Friday." Yes, orange is their corporate color, and on Fridays, they set up popcorn machines, snacks, and games in their breakrooms for all their employees to enjoy. Other ideas can be as simple as managers doing the cooking, serving, and cleanup at company barbecues and picnics. Consider establishing a yearlong calendar of celebrations with a different theme every month. Ice cream socials and pizza are items that bring employees together and make them smile.

Finally, don't forget about your remote workers. You just might have to get creative. Technology can help. A colleague told me about the time her team was spread out over three states. It was holiday time, and they were a little jealous of the local groups that were planning potlucks and Secret Santa grab bags. So they came up with the idea of partying by teleconferencing. They each pulled a Secret Santa name, shipped gifts in advance, and planned virtual potlucks. They couldn't share the taste of food, but they showed it on camera and exchanged recipes. They all ate together at the same time on camera and told stories and jokes. And they all agreed that it was one of the best teambuilding activities they had ever participated in.

## Recognize and Reward Culture Champions

"There is more hunger for love and appreciation in this world than for bread," said Mother Theresa. It is a profound statement taken by itself, but when applied to the world of work, its implications provide wisdom for creating company cultures.

Unfortunately, there is ample research that employees generally do not feel their work is appreciated. According to *Tiny Pulse, The Era of Personal and Peer Accountability, 2015 Employee Engagement and Organizational Culture Report*, "Not even one in three employees feel strongly valued on the job thanks to managers failing to show appreciation, or worse yet, constantly pointing out faults."[36]

Not only will underappreciating your employees likely impact their day-to-day performance, it will also likely impact the way they interact with your customers. Sir Richard Branson, CEO of Virgin, seems to agree. "I have always believed that the way you treat your employees is the way they will treat your customers, and that people flourish when they are praised."

One of the most potent ways to drive your values and reinforce them is through regular recognition of employees who live them. Such recognition is particularly meaningful when it is peer-driven rather than manager-driven. Create simple ways for employees to recognize each other for living your values. This can be built into all-hands meetings, included on your intranet, or you can go very low tech and create a "wall of fame" or postings on bulletin boards. And don't forget team recognition.

Variety is an important element of your reward and recognition strategies, as well as making them meaningful, frequent, and democratic.

---

As we have seen, culture change is hard—sustaining it is even harder. Culture change should not be thought of as a program that is conceptualized, installed, and considered done. Doing so—thinking of it as a sprint—will almost assure that the company becomes a part of the 70 percent of companies that fail in their change initiatives.

Instead of thinking of it as a sprint, think of it as a marathon that is tied to company values, includes ongoing employee involvement, and changes over time—just as the terrain on a marathon course changes across the miles. I have given you a roadmap for long-term success. Now let's turn our attention to some special considerations that arise in today's business world—beginning with the increasing focus on the need for diversity in the workplace and the impact and needs of the millennial generation.

# 10

# Diversity and Millennials

*A company is only as good as the people it keeps.*
–Mary Kay Ash, Founder, Mary Kay Cosmetics

It's unlikely that the founder of the Mary Kay Cosmetics empire was the first to say that a company is only as good as the people it keeps. In some form, this statement has been made many times and in many ways. Elon Musk, CEO of Tesla, Inc., has a perspective that also rings true. "A company is a group organized to create a product or service, and it is only as good as its people and how excited they are about creating." It really is all about the people.

Fundamentally, any enterprise is dependent on the team of individuals who comprise its workforce. You can have the best product in the world, the most innovative service, and a ground-breaking, earth-shattering solution. But it will all be for naught if you don't have the people who can implement for you, people who share your mission and values, people who take pride in what they do and enthusiastically come to work every day.

Alan Tecktiel of Baker McKenzie puts it like this: "The companies that truly get it focus their time and energy on maximizing the potential of their employees, bringing everyone to the table, providing experiences and training that benefit not only the company but the employees as well. People want to have a feeling of moving forward rather than being stagnant—and the companies that understand that will invest in those things." Investing in people will keep you moving past the plateau.

Many companies have realized that the way to get good people is to actually treat them as if they're good people. Show them that they matter. Find out what's important to them and build that into the business.

A prime example of a company that has shifted focus due to massive culture change is Microsoft since Satya Nadella took over as CEO in 2014. He says his job was to create a culture where the smart, the talented, and the passionate can rise to the top. In his book *Hit Refresh*, Nadella emphasizes the importance of the CEO as instigator and manager of culture. "The CEO is the curator of an organization's culture. Anything is possible for a company when its culture is about listening, learning, and harnessing individual passions and talents to the company's mission."[37]

When you're building your organization and defining or refining your culture, it's essential to keep pace with the needs of your employees and customers. Their needs have shifted in the last decade. Our world and our corporate environment have seen dramatic changes in recent years, in particular with regard to ethnicity, gender, and age demographics. Companies that succeed will respond to increasing workforce diversity as well as to the generational ascendency of the millennials. So let's explore these two categories.

## Diversity

A corporate culture that embraces diversity means your company is in sync with the market you serve. Our country is a complex and diverse blend of races, ethnicities, religions, genders, sexual orientations, and generations. Your organization should be the same.

Think of it this way: You need to include, not exclude. You need to embrace the contrasting perspectives of varying work and life experiences. Why? For one thing, having a culture that embraces diversity is essential for success. Diversity not only generates an atmosphere that encourages far-sighted, broadly-based, open-minded creativity and innovation, it also drives bottom-line results.

The findings of a McKinsey study that explored diversity in 180 publicly traded companies in the US, UK, France, and Germany were startlingly consistent. Companies whose executive boards had the most diversity showed returns on equity (ROE) that were 53 percent higher than those that were the least diverse. Earnings before interest and taxes (EBIT) were 14 percent higher.[38]

In spite of such compelling financial results, most companies are lagging when it comes to diversity in leadership. At the end of 2017, only 6.4 percent of Fortune 500 CEOs were women.[39] There were four black chief executives—all men. And there were one Asian woman and one Hispanic woman. The number of women holding Fortune 500 board seats actually declined by 2 percent between 2015 and 2016, while 197 of the top S&P 500 companies had no black directors, according to *Black Enterprise* magazine.[40]

One encouraging sign is that a study by the Institutional Shareholder Services showed that in the first five months of 2018, women accounted for 31 percent of new board directors among the US's three thousand biggest publicly-traded companies. That's a positive development because women previously occupied only 18 percent of such seats. But only 10 percent of lead directors and 4 percent of board chairs are women. This is problematic because, as Laurence D. Fink, Chairman and CEO of BlackRock, told those attending a conference, "If we are not a mirror of who our clients are, we're going to fail."

But it goes beyond that. Microsoft's Nadella believes that to serve the planet (which is not only a part of Microsoft's mission, but probably reflects one of the goals of many companies), the company's makeup needs to reflect that of the planet. And for Microsoft, that includes a diversity of opinions and perspectives.

A business that's ahead of the pack is Adidas, one of the top-performing companies in the McKinsey study and the second-largest sportswear manufacturer in the world. Adidas "designated diversity as a strategic goal and started building it into the guts of the organization."[41] In particular, the company focused on stepping up the number of women in management ranks, and within three years, they saw an increase from 21 percent to 30 percent. Today, Adidas considers diversity so important to how it wants to "invent the future of sport" that it considers diversity its secret formula for that. "The more unique identities, backgrounds and perspectives we can assemble at Adidas, the easier it is to find our way around roadblocks and change lives through the sports we love."[42]

The company's commitment to diversity is reflected at its world headquarters, which boasts employees of eighty nationalities and where the male-female employee ratio is 50-50. It has also been ranked as a leading LGBT-friendly company.

Karen Parkin, Adidas Executive Board Member, Global Human Resources, says, "The level of innovation in any organization is in direct proportion to the diversity of its people. Diversity provides a steady stream of new ideas, fresh perspectives, and contrary points of view that are the lifeblood of innovation."

It's a view that Intel Corporation backs by putting its money where its mouth is with a commitment to spend $300 million to increase diversity in its workforce—the largest such investment by a tech company. In 2015, CEO Brian Krzanich pledged that by the year 2020, Intel's US workforce would mirror the talent available in the country. They see diversity and innovation as not only being the right thing to do but as good for business.[43]

Diversity and inclusion, insists Danielle Brown, Intel's Chief Diversity and Inclusion Officer, can't be an initiative that is buried in HR. It must be an integral part of culture and part of everything the company does. In 2017, Intel set and met its goal of achieving 45 percent diversity in its new hires, specifically women and unrepresented minorities. Intel recognized that "like likes like"—the fundamental human inclination to naturally hire or promote people that share the same characteristics. And it set out to engineer such bias out of those processes.[44]

Like Intel, energy giant Exelon Corporation is putting financial muscle into diversity and has hit the milestone of $2 billion a year in direct spending with minority and women-owned businesses. In 2017, it became the first energy company to join the Billion Dollar Roundtable for Excellence in Supplier Diversity.

The year in which the company did more business with diverse and women-owned businesses was the same year it experienced its best-ever financial performance. This is no surprise. Emmett Vaughn, Director of Diverse Business Empowerment at Exelon, says that there is a relationship between diversity and success.

As we can see, diversity in the workplace is not some feel-good, politically correct goal. It opens doors, facilitates communication, and broadens both perspective and thought. And most important for any resistant naysayers, it stimulates solid financial results.

Exelon's Emmett Vaughn says that executives at the $35 billion energy provider have posed this question: Am I smarter because I read four different newspapers or because I read one newspaper four times? The compelling answer is this: "The more ways you have to expand your perspectives and attack business objectives the more likely you are to have a better outcome."

Vaughn cites the story of Jackie Robinson who broke the color barrier in Major League Baseball when the Brooklyn Dodgers started him at first base in April 1946. Baseball was not broken in the eyes of baseball fans. There was a vibrant Negro League and no big clamor for integration. "But who could imagine writing the history of Major League Baseball today without what has happened thanks to integration? People had no idea how great it could be," says

Vaughn. "So if that is a valid premise, fast forward and apply it to a business organization and see the level of excellence you can achieve when you optimize as many perspectives as you can."

Perhaps we will not need to consciously plan diversity into our companies one day because it will already be so rooted and integrated in company values and cultures that it is second nature. Until then, most organizations need to consider how to increase their diversity.

## How to Increase Diversity

Many companies will tell you they are actively seeking diversity while doing no more than paying lip service to the concept. But it's not difficult to introduce. Below are some tips for driving more diversity in your own organization:

- **Analyze Your Strengths and Gaps:** Are their certain jobs, departments, or business units that are well balanced and diverse? How did they get that way? What are they doing to sustain the diversity they have?

- **Look at the Communities in Which You Operate:** How well does your workforce reflect the world in which you operate?

- **Closely Examine Your Hiring Processes:** Many organizations rely heavily on employee referrals, and with good reason. Employee referrals often deliver great candidates who are a culture and skill fit. But if your workforce is not diverse, employee referrals will perpetuate that situation. Tap into community outreach and other nonprofit programs as a source for candidates, and encourage volunteerism at these organizations. Get in front of university diversity groups if you do a lot of college recruiting.

- **Create Opportunities:** Look for ways to regularly involve diverse talent from your team on important projects.

- **Encourage Mentorships and Sponsorships:** Encourage employees to find mentors and sponsors to help them develop their skills, and encourage your leaders to be mentors and sponsors. Get employees and leaders thinking about talent on an ongoing basis. Mentors help employees evaluate their careers and what they need to develop. Sponsors help them make it happen.

- **Provide Diversity Training:** Educate employees and managers on the bottom-line value of diversity—and how to support it. Consider bringing in an outside diversity expert to provide this if it is not an area of expertise in your HR team.

- **Focus on Retention:** First, do your diverse hires stay? Crunch the numbers. If not, find out why.

- **Empower Employees to Form Affinity Groups:** Think of affinity groups as an internal networking process. These are safe places for employees to share common interests and support each other. Sometimes called employee or resource groups, they have been mainstays of many organizations to help recruit, develop, and retain diverse candidates.

- **Measure Your Progress:** Track changes in diversity in your leadership ranks. This is not only a way to measure what you are doing but also provides great data for attracting more talent to your organization.

- **Invest in the Future:** Millennials represent the most diverse workforce we have seen. Develop programs that focus on their values and needs.

# Millennials

Self-absorbed? Obsessed with tech? Entitled? Flaky? Selfish? Job-hoppers?

Opinions about the millennial generation are often not complimentary, but it's a generation that can't be ignored. Millennials are fast approaching nearly half the working population. Their desires will be pivotal in driving the culture in every industry. A hallmark of the millennials is the value they place on company culture, much more so than any previous generation.

## *Social Consciousness*

Millennials are socially responsible and cause-driven. It's not all about the money, and it's very much about the contribution they can make. A company that espouses such values and believes in making a difference is somewhere they will call home. Sweeping generalizations? Not at all. Look first from the consumer side. Millennials brandish about $2.5 trillion in spending power and, according to Cone Communications, 70 percent of them prefer to award their money to brands that support causes they care about.[45] They're a force to be reckoned with. But those consumers are also employees—and they take the same attitude into the workplace.

Several studies have shown that millennials desire purpose in their work as well as in their overall life. In one study, a whopping 94 percent of them declared they wanted to use their skills for a social good.[46] And a Fidelity Investments study revealed that millennials were even happy to take a pay cut of $7,600, on average, in return for a job that provided more purposeful work, better work-life balance, or a better company culture.[47]

A University of North Carolina (UNC) Kenan-Flagler Business School report titled "Maximizing Millennials in the Workplace" says, "This generation is socially conscious and expects their employers to act in socially conscious ways. For them, work isn't just about income, it's about personal enrichment and fulfillment, which means that having flexibility in their work schedules is highly regarded."[48]

### Desire Flexibility

Yes, millennials love flexibility: where they work, what they work on, and when they work.

Once regarded as a soft perk for employees, "the truth is dramatically more comprehensive than that for both employees and employers," says 1 Million for Work Flexibility, an organization that has launched a national initiative in support of work flexibility.

Employees enjoy a better work/life balance, less stress, time saved from the rigors of commuting, and healthier relationships when there is work flexibility. Employers benefit with increased productivity, financial savings, reduced turnover, less absenteeism, and an overall more positive corporate culture. Other benefits of flexibility, says 1 Million for Work Flexibility, are just as meaningful, if not so obvious: boosting rural economies, supporting military vets, and creating career opportunities for the disabled.

The popularity of telecommuting is growing dramatically. A US Census Bureau report in September 2018 showed that about eight million people work from home, making telecommuting the second most common way to get to work, second only to driving and ahead of public transportation for the first time. The actual number is probably even higher because the census survey asked how respondents "usually" go to work. A 2016 Gallup survey found that 43 percent of employees spend at least some time working remotely.

Workplace flexibility is more than telecommunication and flexible schedules. It is a powerful way to support and enhance diversity. When employee needs are met, we improve retention of the diverse group we worked so hard to source and hire in the first place. Effective workplaces are not one-size-fits-all, and the most successful companies are creatively recognizing this. Benefits offered include time off for volunteering, health insurance for unmarried partners, caregiving time off, and reduced work schedules. According to the Society for Human Resource Management (SHRM), small employers are big leaders in workplace flexibility and more likely to offer traditional flextime, control over breaks, and time off to attend to personal issues.

While the move to work from home may originally have been led by workers, companies are increasingly encouraging the trend, especially with an increasing number of tech-oriented jobs that can be performed anywhere. A FlexJobs report found the number of home-based workers has skyrocketed by 115 percent over the past decade, and some experts predict that half of all full-time workers could soon be working remotely.

### Need a Reason to Stay or They're Gone

If you don't give millennials reasons to stay, they're fast to move on. The Fidelity Investments study indicated that millennials are often eager to make a move, with 41 percent expecting to start a new job in the next two years. The same conclusion was reached in a 2016 Gallup poll, "How Millennials Want to Work and Live,"[49] which reported that 21 percent of millennials had changed jobs within the prior year—more than three times the number from other generations. Gallup estimated that such turnover costs the U.S. economy $30.5 billion annually.

But job-hopping is not necessarily a bad thing, says Eileen Benwitt, Chief Talent Officer at Horizon Media. "If you get two to three years out of a millennial, I consider that a success. Their value comes after years of varying experiences and roles, so to stay in one place for too long doesn't always serve either the employee or the company."

Some millennials, she says, even boomerang back to you with new, interesting perspectives that contribute to the company in ways they could never have done before.

Is it the "restlessness" of millennials that's to blame for job-hopping, or is it the corporate culture? Gallup looks at it this way: "It's possible that many millennials actually don't want to switch jobs, but their companies aren't giving them compelling reasons to stay. When millennials see what appears to be a better opportunity, they have every incentive to take it. While millennials can come across as wanting more and more, the reality is that they just want a job that feels worthwhile—and they will keep looking until they find it."[50]

But if retention is your focus, consider research by the Great Place to Work Institute that says the most important thing you can do is build a high-trust culture. "You might find some initial benefits to ditching your dress code and throwing out cubicles," says Chinwe Onyeagoro, the Institute's president. "But superficial changes like these won't improve retention among millennials unless they're accompanied by managers making authentic connections with employees, linking their work and contributions to a broader purpose, providing access to a diverse array of learning and development opportunities, and demonstrating fairness in promotion and advancement decisions."

## Technology-Impacted

There's no doubt that millennials have grown up in a technologically advanced era that their parents never dreamed about. "They are tech-savvy multitaskers because that is all they have ever known. Millennials crave collaboration, team-based work projects and an unstructured flow of information at all levels," says the UNC report.

One of the challenges, though, is that the digital upbringing has led to an attention span that is easily shifted and causes short-term thinking. Millennials are constantly stimulated by tech, so they think that what's happening right now is the most important thing. As one millennial executive in the financial sector told me, "It's hard to think long-term and strategically when you're responding to too much stimuli." Looking to the future, he says, "A world of senior leaders with shorter memory and attention span is scary."

Wil Reynolds of Seer Interactive empathizes with millennials. Social media and other tools have given them the ability to compare themselves not just to the peers around them but to others globally. He says that for earlier generations, keeping up with the Joneses meant comparing oneself to ten or twenty Joneses. But with Facebook and Instagram, millennials might be trying to keep up with three thousand Joneses. "The impression might be that everyone else is doing something fun and exciting. But it's a misrepresentation based on seeing a handful of posts. Not everyone is on vacation, they've just seen the photos of those who are! The other three thousand aren't posting photos of themselves sitting at their desks," says Reynolds.

According to Gallup, though, only 29 percent of millennials are engaged at work, possibly because during the recession, they had to take jobs just to pick up a paycheck. Worse still, 16 percent of millennials are *actively disengaged*, which means their negativity could seriously damage the company. Says Gallup, "The millennial workforce is predominantly 'checked out'—not putting energy or passion into their jobs. Not engaging millennials is a big miss for organizations."

### Engaging with Millennials

So, what to do?

Managers should make every effort to connect with their employees every day. It doesn't have to be a thirty-minute meeting or even a ten-minute meeting. A quick call, a drop by for a few minutes, or just a couple of brief texts is sufficient. There needs to be more constant, ongoing feedback in small and varied ways. Keep communication flowing. Be open and transparent.

Millennials crave feedback from their managers, probably because they've come of age in an era of remarkable connectedness, in a digital age in which they have engaged in a constant feedback loop. The problem is that more often than not, they don't get feedback. Only 19 percent say they receive routine feedback. But in many ways, they're just as much to blame as those not giving that frequent feedback. They want it, but they don't ask for it. Managers should take the initiative and remind them that it is okay to ask.

A great way to provide feedback and support is through mentoring. In fact, a strong mentoring program not only provides the support these less experienced employees need, it is also a great way to reengage seasoned, long-term employees. We worked closely with a large, legacy engineering and manufacturing company in central Pennsylvania on just such a program. They were struggling with rapid and costly turnover of their recent college grad hires. At the same time, their baby boomer engineers, many of whom were planning to retire in five to seven years, were becoming disengaged. Not only did many of these employees need to be reengaged, there was also the challenge of capturing their twenty-five-plus years of experience and knowledge.

They decided to develop these engineers into mentors, working first with the college grads. We developed and delivered a two-day mentor training program and followed up with bi-monthly online discussions. Not only did new hire turnover decrease, but the mentors were reengaged. They felt valued and enjoyed working with the "young people." They learned as much from their mentees as the mentees learned from them. In surveys, the mentees reported how helpful it had been to learn the ropes, understand the unwritten rules about how to get things done, get advice on how to grow their careers, and so on. They were also very proud of how they had helped their mentors better understand technology.

Feedback needs to be constant and ongoing, not once a year. Companies like Deloitte, Adobe, Accenture, and General Electric have already taken the lead in ditching annual review processes because they feel they are ineffective. Says Gallup, "Employees need more than check-the-box evaluations, and millennials are leading the way for this change."[51]

"Transparency is key," says Auto Club's Chris Baggaley. "We need to be transparent with employees and allow them to be transparent with us. Leaders should be open to employees coming to us with problems and address issues in a constructive way. This point would be well-taken by any company wanting to transform its culture. If there is an unwritten company rule that bringing up bad news will be taken badly by leadership, then people simply will not speak up. And if they don't speak up, problems can remain opaque for a long time. This is especially true when it comes to millennials.

## Pulling It All Together: KONE

When you think of an elevator company, you probably don't think about much more than its ability to get you from the ground floor to the penthouse floor. But don't tell that to the KONE Corporation, a global leader in the elevator and escalator industry.

KONE's mission is to "improve the flow of urban life" making "people's journeys safe, convenient and reliable in taller, smarter buildings." It's in the business of "vertical transportation." Or put another way, it is in the people-flow business rather than the elevator and escalator business.

And the next time you're riding in a KONE elevator or escalator consider this: You're among a billion people worldwide doing the same thing that same day. Their ultimate customer, says Steve Gonzalez, Director, Major Projects Unit, Americas, is anyone who enters a high-rise building, an airport, a subway station, or anywhere that people travel. But, of course, their customers are also the people who design and develop buildings, build buildings, and own buildings.

KONE's culture, says Gonzalez, is one of innovation, commitment, and curiosity. Its innovative prowess, helping cities to become better places in which to live, has been acknowledged by Forbes in its "World's Most Innovative Companies" list seven years in a row. The company has an innovation portal where it captures the great ideas of employees.

KONE also has a culture of commitment, both to their customers and to their employees. Employee safety is a part of that commitment. "Construction is a very dangerous business, and we work very hard to make sure our employees and everyone using our equipment go home safely every day." Regular face-to-face meetings all start with a safety discussion.

"Yes, we have a culture of curiosity," says Gonzalez. "We have many steering committees and ad hoc meetings to evaluate opportunities and brainstorm new approaches." KONE also brings people in from all over the country and sometimes from all over the world for trainings.

In 2017, KONE had annual net sales of over $10 billion with more than fifty-five thousand employees, and it strives to avoid the plateau that impacts so many large companies. One of their innovative strategies to avoid stagnation is to hire people from other industries who haven't been involved in the elevator business. These recruits, therefore, don't have entrenched views of the industry and bring fresh problem-solving perspectives.

Gonzalez highly recommends the same kind of healthy open-minded approach for any large company: "It's valuable to look at companies other than those you typically regard as your competitors because chances are they're experiencing the same problems you are. Look outside that circle for potential solutions." Chances are when you research what companies in divergent industries are doing, you'll find some innovative answers. And be prepared to take dramatic action: "Sometimes you need revolution to get evolution."

In addition, Gonzalez stresses teamwork and diversity, especially important for a company that has one thousand offices in over fifty countries.

Added Gonzalez, "We bring people in from all over the world to accomplish a common goal. We operate in many countries, and these countries are melting pots just like the States. And when you think about it, a construction site is a microcosm of a country." At one site in particular, the development of the Marina Bay Sands Resort and Casino in Singapore, the KONE team was part of twenty thousand workers from numerous countries who all needed to coordinate to get the job done.

Diversity also includes different generations and recognizing the differing needs of each. Take millennials, for example. Gonzalez points out that technology is intuitive for many millennials because they've grown up with it. That makes them far more comfortable with it than some in the older generation. And millennials, says Gonzalez, bring a new attitude to the work environment. "Millennials certainly operate well in an environment where people are committed to people."

For your business to be in sync with the times—and your customer base—considering the makeup of your talent is critical. For many (maybe most) companies, that means making sure not only that you have a workforce that is diverse and includes millennials but that you have a culture that attracts and retains them.

As stated earlier, diversity not only generates an atmosphere that encourages far-sighted, broadly-based, open-minded creativity and innovation, but also drives bottom-line results. Diversity is not a buzzword, it is a smart way to do business and a key driver of success.

Increasingly, corporate leaders have recognized the millennial generation's unique competencies and perspectives and know they need to harness their strengths. Millennials are not the future, they are the now. Leaders need to understand what drives them if they want to tap in to the fastest-growing generation in the workplace. According to Pew Research Center, millennials are "relatively unattached to organized politics and religion, linked by social media, burdened by debt, distrustful of people, in no rush to marry—and optimistic about the future."[52]

All of these factors need to be taken into account to create a thriving culture to take your company into the future. What also needs to be taken into account in today's market is the shrinking world that has been created by globalization, technology, and mergers and acquisitions. And that is something we're going to look at next.

# Global Considerations, Mergers, and Technology

*"We are living through the most profound changes in the economy since the Industrial Revolution. Technology, globalization, and the accelerating pace of change have yielded chaotic markets, fierce competition, and unpredictable staff requirements."*
–Bruce Tulgan, author of *Not Everyone Gets a Trophy*

What happens when the culture of the world's largest online retailer connects with the unique culture of a major bricks-and-mortar grocery chain? In the summer of 2017, that became a reality when internet goliath Amazon (annual revenues approaching $200 billion) acquired for $13.7 billion the 473 stores of Whole Foods, the supermarket enterprise that bills itself as "America's healthiest grocery store."

Martin Bullis, Coordinator/Director for Whole Foods Markets in the Greater Chicago area, discussed the impact with me. "Culturally, we are completely different from Amazon," he said. "They move at a much faster pace."

But perhaps most significantly, whereas Amazon is a global undertaking, Whole Foods has made a big emphasis on forging an identity with local communities. They focus on local culture and local markets. They hire and source products locally. "We act as a local catalyst because we care about the community," said Bullis.

Whole Foods has always been a company that listens to its employees, from directors to frontline cashiers. "A key aspect of Whole Foods culture is respect for the individual. I was at a meeting where someone had a bright-red Mohawk and army boots. It's about who we are, not what we look like. It's about what we do and who is important—and that's the customer. This is why we are a good fit with Jeff Bezos."

The online giant made the merger easier by working collaboratively with Whole Foods. Bullis provided a specific example of Amazon's approach: the way a suspected data breach was handled. Amazon provided guidance to help identify how it happened and how to take the right steps to make sure it didn't happen again. Not only did Amazon share their expertise, but they did so without assuming that all of their recommendations would work in the Whole Foods environment—true collaboration.

Another major element of the merger with Amazon was getting the team leaders in individual stores to appreciate the benefits. "It was an educational process. We needed them to understand the big picture in terms of improving the overall business. And how to collaborate," said Bullis. "I didn't come in here as a change agent, but that's what my role turned out to be. In a way, working with Amazon was just like working with another region of Whole Foods—a question of relationship-building."

## Going Global

The world is shrinking. Change has gone from fast to hyper-paced. International markets are opening up, and it's easier than ever before for a company to expand beyond its own borders. Technology, in particular, has helped level the playing field for smaller businesses, empowering entrepreneurs to operate in the big leagues. We're connected in ways that were totally unimaginable just a few years ago.

Because of that, corporate culture is a more important consideration than it has ever been. For companies to grow and move beyond the plateau, it's essential to be fully aware of the risks and rewards of global expansion, the challenges of merging with other companies whose culture is vastly different, and how rapidly-evolving technological advances change everything.

Let's start with a company that needs no introduction, a company that is truly global, operating in more than 160 countries: Xerox. Bala Sathyanarayanan calls its approach to culture "Glo-calization." What does that mean? It means that while a company has one identity wherever it ventures in the world, it has to be adaptable, making allowances for geographical differences and cultures while building and shaping the corporate culture.

"Headquarters has the job of defining the company's mission, purpose, and values, but employees in Sri Lanka, Latvia, Nigeria, or wherever must be given the flexibility of interpreting those values and purpose in a way that will enable them to connect with the company's clients and employees in that country," Sathyanarayanan told me. More specifically, he says that many cultures—global, country, department, and individual—must come into alignment.

Sathyanarayanan sings the praises of GE, who owns Xerox, with regard to the multinational conglomerate's model for building shared company values. At its learning center in Ossining, New York, GE hosts as many as twelve thousand employees every year from all over the world who make the trip to get steeped in management skills and the corporate culture. Employees have an opportunity to network and build lifelong relationships that serve them well as they move through the ranks. When they return to their countries, they return fully immersed in the GE culture.

Sathyanarayanan points to particular issues that arise when considering cultural differences from country to country. One of those issues is the fact that you cannot compare millennials from the US with those in other parts of the world. The cultures, life experiences, and opportunities are different in different parts of the world, so even though a person from the US and a person from China may both be millennials, those differences must be taken into consideration.

Likewise, gender diversity is something that cannot be separated from country and culture. "Gender diversity becomes a major problem depending on the country we are operating in," says Sathyanarayanan. "But even still, if there is an opening for a position in Saudi Arabia, for example, we make sure women are able to interview."

Further, the cultures of some countries—like Japan—are less risk-oriented than the US. This is something that has a significant impact on the way negotiations are conducted, decisions are made, ideas are communicated, and success is achieved.

Sathyanarayanan's view is echoed by Chubb, the world's largest publicly traded property and casualty insurer with operations in fifty-four countries. "We value local talent because without them, it is not possible to understand local market practices and business customs. Having local talent is a key reason we are successful," Justin Boyson, Director and Far East Regional Vice President, Personal Lines, told me.

When Chubb moves into another country, they seek companies that can provide expanded business opportunities through improved product, distribution, and talent. But they also seek companies that have similar business practices and underwriting discipline to facilitate integration. "When working internationally, nothing is cookie-cutter, and it is important to understand and learn from local country leaders. Products and services that may work well in the US, for example, may not be accepted by the local marketplace because of local regulation, culture, or product knowledge. This is why local know-how is so crucial," Boyson said.

Chubb constantly seeks collaboration from team members across different levels of expertise and geographies. Not only does that help to eliminate a top-down mentality, it also ensures that local market, customer, and operations issues and nuances are taken into account.

At Emerson Automation Solutions, the approach is to hire people who fit the Emerson culture. Tony Norris, Vice President, Global Sales for Rosemount Flame and Gas products within Emerson, acknowledges that different countries have different cultural norms, but that for those who work at Emerson, it is the Emerson culture—and its company emphasis on ethics—that is the driver, not the local culture.

Similar thinking is present at thyssenkrupp North America, which is part of the German diversified industrial company that focuses on engineering. More than forty companies operate in the US, Canada, and Mexico under the thyssenkrupp umbrella and have contributed to projects such as the engineering and installation of elevators and escalators within the One World Trade Center Building and Memorial site. It's a very diverse company, but thyssenkrupp is trying to build a unified culture. "We are trying to create one message platform and one culture so we can drive the business forward," Senior Vice President of Communications Jonathan Evans told me. Evans believes that doing this includes placing trust in their people and avoiding micromanaging them. The object is to help them get the job done well and be successful. And as he points out, "If people are successful, organizations tend to be successful."

## Mergers and Acquisitions

Mergers and acquisitions (M&As) are a time-honored method to expand a business entity—so much so that companies dish out more than $2 trillion a year acquiring other companies. The word *marriage* is thrown around a lot when the coming together of two corporate entities is discussed. But the bitter truth is that there is often not much love involved, and the ugliness of divorce frequently enters the picture.

While 40 percent to 50 percent of marriages between people don't survive, astonishingly, numerous studies show that anywhere between 70 percent and 90 percent of corporate marriages end in failure.

And the number one reason for corporate marriage failure is culture clash: two different mindsets, two different ways of operating, two different aspirations. Or as Don Harrison, developer of the Accelerating Implementation Methodology (AIM), so neatly expresses it, "Same beds, different dreams."

In fact, culture clash was the primary reason for failure in more than half of thousands of acquisitions studied by Vector Group, a global consulting firm.[53] Many company leaders just don't give enough consideration to the challenges posed by effecting a merger. They focus on exciting potential increases in revenue, bottom-line profit, or increase in market share. But the "culture thing" is treated as the unwanted stepchild. It's plain ignored and taken for granted. Even worse, a McKinsey survey reported the shocking statistic that 29 percent of executives said their companies were just "not willing to make changes or launch targeted interventions to address cultural gaps."[54]

And even when they see the need, Alan J. Smith, CEO of M&A consulting firm Bay Pacific Group, says, "Executives underestimate the challenge involved in successfully blending corporate cultures."

A corollary to the challenge of blending cultures is the challenge of merging the talent bases of two companies. Often, there is a lack of planning and even blatant disregard of assessing and blending the merging companies' talent bases. Doing so runs the risk of losing the best people on both sides. To illustrate these points, let's look at some historical examples of M&As gone bad and the reasons why they have done so.[55]

- **German vs American Culture:** The union of auto manufacturers Daimler (makers of Mercedes-Benz) and

Chrysler in the late 1990s was hailed as a "merger of equals." But the German operating culture quickly dominated the American culture, and Chrysler employee satisfaction levels plummeted. In 2007, Daimler acknowledged its error and sold Chrysler to a capital management firm.

- **New Media vs Old Media:** The $350 billion merger of Time Warner and AOL proved disastrous. In January 2000, Time Warner stock was $71.88 a share. Eight years later it was under $15.00. Richard Parsons, president of Time Warner, confessed that he underestimated just how different the company cultures were. "It was beyond my abilities to figure out how to blend the old media and the new media culture."

- **Engineering vs Sales:** Computer giant Hewlett Packard took over Compaq in 2001 when both companies were struggling. But their cultures were miles apart. HP was regarded as an engineering-driven culture, based on consensus, while the Compaq sales-driven culture was based on rapid decision-making. Years of bitter infighting led to a $13 billion loss in market capitalization.

- **Entrepreneurial vs Traditional:** In the highly competitive telecom market of 2005, Sprint, while battling industry leaders Verizon and AT&T, acquired Nextel in a $35 billion deal—only to write down its valuation three years later. As entrepreneur Darcy Jacobsen described it, "That failure is widely attributed to a culture clash between the entrepreneurial, khaki culture of Nextel and the buttoned-down formality of bureaucratic Sprint." When Sprint disposed itself of Nextel in 2012, CNET called it "a concluding hapter in one of the worst mergers in history."

## Blending Corporate Cultures

What can you do to smoothly blend corporate cultures? Plan ahead, because the early days of a merger are the most precarious. This is the time when employees on both sides are most nervous about the relationship and how it is going to play out.[56] How can you bring two cultures together to build a joint organization that's stronger by uniting?

First, define the culture you want. Jointly establish your core values. If you don't know what they are, you can't expect employees to get it.

Second, research and identify any significant cultural differences. Interview relevant personnel, hold focus groups, and conduct employee surveys. Talk to customers. They will be impacted too.

Third, communicate with employees, new and old. Keep them informed about progress. Make them feel involved. Foster links between peers at the two companies. Be ready to respond quickly to the inevitable rumors and concerns. As Nielsen's Chris Augustine told me, "When employees aren't sure of what to expect next, it can leave everyone on edge, waiting for the other shoe to drop. This is especially true during mergers or acquisitions, when facts and plans aren't being shared freely, leaving the employee base to come up with their own conclusions—whether they are right or wrong."

Fourth, plug the brain drain. Often, key managers become disenchanted with the blending of two companies. Go out of your way to keep this influential group on board. Otherwise, an exodus of talent can spread throughout the ranks. Make sure people from both sides of the merger are involved in key projects.

Fifth, as I stated earlier, don't forget that a company is only as good as its people. Companies often focus on integrating the operational elements (the policies and procedures, rules and regulations), but don't give equal time to the human elements (the relationships and informal structures). Conduct talent reviews sooner rather than later and identify the "keepers." An executive from Coca-Cola once told me, "Identify your top talent and get your arms around them. Show them the love, over and over." Sage advice, indeed.

Sixth, size matters. The smaller your company, the greater the chances you think you can't afford to devote resources to the issue of merging cultures. Don't short-change culture. Smaller companies are more intimate environments, and because of that, the consequences of ignoring the issue of culture or thinking it will take care of itself can be extremely damaging.

John Hren, business director for a multinational basic minerals and marketing company, has seen corporate mergers from both sides of the fence. In one experience, one of the merging companies was very focused on short-term profits, cash flow, and the marketing program, while the other company's culture was much more focused on the long-term investment and basic research. "It almost turned into a civil war," he recalled. Figuring out how they were all going to get along consumed the organization.

What lessons did he learn? "If you don't set out a strong harmonious vision early in the merger process, it just degenerates into individual fiefdoms. If you don't have a vision that both sides believe in and can work towards, then you're already a step behind." The vision has to be authentic and effectively communicated if you want employees from both merging companies to truly buy into it, he said. And it's vital to get quick wins. "Get both sides focused on tasks and sub-tasks that can be achieved quickly. Having common goals to focus on—and completing them side by side—helps to bring the two different cultures together in the early stages."

McKinsey's Jennifer Speciale also gave me an excellent example from her personal experience working for a company that was acquired by an entity whose culture was "completely antithetical." One of her designers, she said, came in from a client meeting with the new company, lay down on the floor, "did a superman," and cried because the cultures were so different.

Then there was an unforgettable conference call when they were told all of their designers would have to turn in their beloved Macs because they only used IBM laptops. She was horrified. "The Mac is not a handbag. It's a tool of the trade. It's vital for creative and productive work."

Speciale says she learned a lot trying to bridge the two cultures. "Each side thought there were many things about the other side that was ridiculous." That experience made her nervous about building her own group at McKinsey until she decided that it had to be easier to build a group organically than acquire people through acquisitions.

While that's certainly true, doing effective "cultural due diligence" can avoid culture clash. Gary W. Craig, Managing Partner and COO for Vector Group, says that in over thirty years of handling M&As across the world, he's never seen two organizational cultures that could not be successfully integrated. "M&A failure due to culture clash is just a way of describing management negligence, arrogance, ignorance, or some mix of the three. Dysfunctional culture clash need never occur."

## Technology

The rapid advance of technology has had a seismic impact on the ways companies do business—probably the equivalent of a 9.0 on the Richter scale and clearly destined to continue down that path with no end in sight. Just consider the impact of Wi-Fi, smartphones, tablets, laptops, and social media and the ways they have dramatically changed not only business operations but also business culture. No company can afford to reach a plateau and use outdated technology when the super-computing power of a cellphone sits in the palm of your hand. Every company, regardless of industry, needs to be a tech savvy company to compete.

What are the positives and negatives of the high-tech environment? It's an issue that can't be ignored because technological capabilities will continue to rapidly expand, way beyond those of today and in ways that most of us can't even begin to imagine.

- **Transparency and Democracy:** The digital world enables easy sharing of data that once might have been closely held by top leaders, either out of necessity or arbitrarily. Maybe it was just too cumbersome to distribute throughout the ranks, or maybe the select privileged few wanted to keep it that way as a means of control and power.[57] But now, online chat sessions can permit employees at all levels to quiz senior executives and directly deliver input in ways they never could before. More informed and involved employees equals more engaged and happier employees, which in turn equates to more productive employees.

- **Informality:** Office dress code has changed over the years. In many organizations, casual Friday has become casual every day. It's happening in communications too. Casual (that is, incorrect) grammar and punctuation as well as the use of emojis have begun to permeate organizations. (And I'm not sure that's such a good thing.) But these changes are examples of the way communication is changing corporate culture.

- **Collaboration:** Online shared sites have made collaboration easier than ever. It's possible to share ideas and give feedback, whether it's to a colleague across the hall or across the globe. You can create projects together and track performance. This can also reduce barriers between upper and lower management as well as across cultural divides. Workplaces of the future might be global melting pots, which inevitably transforms a company's culture.

- **Research:** Cloud-based computing gives us instant access to databases within our own companies, no matter where we may be, and from the shelves of the largest libraries anywhere.

- **Freedom:** Freedom? Yes. Employees no longer have to be chained to their desks from 9:00 to 5:00. They don't have to wade through dozens of heavy folders stuffed with paper. They can look up data online, wherever they happen to be. This means an increasing emphasis on remote working and a flexible workplace. It offers the ability to steer clear of a frustrating and nonproductive one-hour commute to the office. While working from home was initially viewed with some skepticism, it is a policy that is being increasing embraced—because it gets results. Working where and when the employee wants to work is becoming part of many corporate cultures. Employers who permit flexible work hours are rewarded with a decrease in absenteeism and employee turnover and an increase in morale and productivity.

So, what's the downside of this hyper-connected techno world? For one thing, a 2011 Pew Research Center survey suggests that employees between the ages of eighteen and twenty-four receive about thirty text messages every day ... *while at work.*[58] We know how those pinging alerts are irresistible, but apart from the time taken to read and respond to them, the distraction from a work project can lead to errors. On the other hand, some kind of ban on texting can make employees feel suffocated, controlled, and resentful. The authors of a Deloitte Insights article provided another sound reason to discourage texting: "With everyone hyper-connected, the reality may be that employees have few opportunities to get away from their devices and spend time thinking and solving problems."[59]

Another downside is that the ubiquity of technology propagates an "always on" work ethic where employers can require employees to answer emails or texts and perform tasks outside of office hours. Employees are either expected to be connected 24/7 or take it upon themselves to be wired-in all the time. This risks employee burnout and disillusionment, especially among millennials, who, in particular, seek a healthy work-life balance. In a 2014 Deloitte survey, 65 percent of executives rated the "overwhelmed employee"—overwhelmed as the result of round-the-clock connectivity—an urgent or important trend.

What's an employer to do? What does today's culture require? Is it a matter of accepting that this is just the way it is, or should we try to implement some kind of phone restrictions? Should we insist that employees have designated downtime when they can disconnect and be free of work concerns? Perhaps issue guidelines on sending emails? Do all those people really need to be cc'd? One trend we see with our clients is no-email Fridays.

We need to be masters of technology, not slaves of technology. Technology is nothing more than a tool. It's how you use that tool that matters. It can be a force for good or bad. It's up to you. More importantly, know how you will use technology. A mastery of it is essential, especially as millennials start to become the majority.

---

There are many challenges to creating and sustaining a robust, healthy culture. Whether your organization is challenged by a growing global presence, complex mergers, or rapid shifts in technology, you need a plan to anticipate such challenges and a strategy to address them.

# A Call to Action

*"Without a sense of purpose, no company, either public
or private, can achieve its full potential."*
–Larry Fink, Chairman & CEO, BlackRock

It's time to spark culture within your organization, time to implement the strategies that will stimulate the development of a company in which everyone is proud of your shared goals and is dedicated to putting them into practice. What is your organization most concerned about? Consider the following list. Which of these challenges keep you and your leadership team up nights? What would you add to this list?

- Uncertainty about the future
- Fiscal integrity and management
- Talent shortages
- Rapid technological change
- Maintaining reputation
- Resistance to change
- Customer loyalty
- Shifting regulation

- Problem solving and risk management
- Globalization
- Diversity
- Information overload

These are the primary challenges I see when my team and I meet with leaders across the US. The key point we stress with them is that leaders need to guide and inspire their teams to perform in challenging, chaotic environments. They need to lead the way to create dynamic, team-oriented organizations where innovation and resiliency thrive—and where the risk failure may be high. Our world is changing at the fastest pace we have ever known, and businesses today fail at an alarmingly fast rate. Failure itself is not a catastrophe, but failing to learn from failure is.

A concept that was incorporated into Army leadership curriculum in 1988 is relevant today for organizations of every stripe. It's VUCA, an acronym that stands for volatility, uncertainty, complexity, and ambiguity. A strong culture that honors trust, honesty, integrity, and respect gives us all the ammunition we need to respond to the challenges of the VUCA environment.

**Volatility:** A shared vision, shared values, and a shared sense of purpose are the cornerstones of a strong culture. They arm us against the volatility of the market and of the world in which we operate. When we all know who we are, why we are in business, and what we stand for, we make better, more consistent decisions, and we can more readily rally the troops.

**Uncertainty:** A strong culture protects against uncertainty. When employees believe in what we do and what we stand for, they are more able to weather the unknown, in large part because they trust leadership to make the right decisions.

**Complexity:** A strong culture reduces complexity. Decision making is easier when we make decisions based on a set of shared norms and values. We know the right thing to do, even when the right thing is also the hardest thing to do.

**Ambiguity:** Culture is a vaccination against the threat of ambiguity. The world in which we work can be very ambiguous, but a strong culture is just the opposite. It knows its purpose.

Organizations that become complacent or lose sight of their purpose are doomed to decline. Organizations need to live their beliefs: Be authentic. Be true to their word. These are values that have always been important, but never more so than today with the rise of the millennial generation and the generations that will soon follow.

The workplace has changed in large part because the workforce has changed. Baby boomers are retiring in droves, and millennials are the core of today's employee base. In fact, they have been the largest generation in the labor force since 2016. Generation Z, those born after 1996, are not far behind. They expect the organizations they work for to have a positive culture, a clearly defined purpose, and clearly articulated and *lived* shared values.

The importance of purpose and shared values is emphasized in the following advice from BlackRock, one of Wall Street's biggest investors, which manages more than $5 trillion in assets worldwide. In a letter to the companies in which it invests, it said, "To prosper over time, every company must not only deliver financial performance, but also show how it makes a positive contribution to society."[60]

Remember also that culture is a key component for attracting and retaining talent. There truly are no great companies without great people, and the competition for talent has never been fiercer. The right culture gives you a competitive edge to attract and retain the kind of people who will take your business forward. The change in attitude is so great that job seekers are now placing a company's culture above all else. A 2017 Korn Ferry survey of over a thousand recruiters found that job candidates are no longer deciding which companies to work for based on the benefits package but on the culture and company purpose.[61]

As the millennial generation assumes leadership positions higher and higher up the corporate ladder, culture, and especially purpose, are increasingly taking center stage. Enhancing quality of life, going green, and helping the disadvantaged—these are causes that were not on the radar of many CEOs a few years ago, but they are now.

And what about brand? More than ever, customers are attracted to brands that they feel align with their own personal beliefs. They buy products and services from organizations they trust and understand. Another Korn Ferry study revealed that purpose-driven consumer products companies greatly outperformed their peers, growing sales at 9.9 percent per year from 2011 to 2015 compared with 2.4 percent growth of those companies not as purpose-driven.[62]

No organization can withstand the buffeting impact of VUCA without a strong, positive culture. Culture shapes our workforce's behaviors and beliefs, their perception of what is important, and their perception of right and wrong. All companies have defined structures and policies, and one organizational chart often looks very much like any other. But culture is as unique as an individual's finger-prints. It is the core set of shared values and norms that characterize each particular company.

You may find organizations that share some or many of your values, you may find certain cultural characteristics in common, but there is no company exactly like your own, and your employees and customers know it. Your culture is your DNA, and your DNA is yours alone. It defines the guidelines, the boundaries, and the dos and don'ts for every action you take and every decision you make. Talented people—whether they are employees, vendors, or clients—want to do business with you in large part because of this DNA, and not simply because of your products or services.

The evidence is clear. Becoming a company with a culture that makes employees want to work for you and customers want to do business with you means you can continue to grow and sustain that growth. The road map I've given you is based on the hands-on experiences of my team and me at Ideal Outcomes. It's based on thorough research into methodologies that work and input from corporate leaders with varied positions working in different sectors. It's a system we've implemented with great success, day in and day out.

To recap the approach: Define, Diagnose, Plan, Measure, and Sustain.

## Define

Clearly state the culture of your organization. Why are you in business? What are your values? If needed, use the sample questions provided for a purpose discussion that leads to the creation of a purpose statement. Communicate the outcome. There's no point developing a statement if you don't effectively tell everyone about it!

## Diagnose

Even if you haven't consciously developed a culture, you have one. It just might not be the right one. So first uncover the culture that you have. Use the Culture Walk Tool. Go around your company and assess the current culture. Use surveys. Remember, your competition can copy your products and even your operations, but emulating your culture is virtually impossible.

## Plan

There are two parts to formulating a plan: aligning your strategy and your processes; and hiring and keeping the right people. Make sure your employee-related processes match your desired culture. Do the same with your customer-related processes. Employ the five essential strategies for talent acquisition and long-term development. Transform your performance management process into a continuing coaching and feedback process.

## Measure

If you do not measure your progress, you cannot expect to achieve the results you desire. Keep measurement of culture simple, and treat culture as you treat any other business initiative. Measure frequently so that you can communicate and celebrate successes along the way.

## Sustain

If you are unable to maintain changes to the culture, explore why. Then employ strategies to ensure that it does not happen again. Those strategies include attending to essential communication, providing values training, creating the role of Chief Culture Officer, and celebrating success.

## A Final Word

Culture is the spark that can light a blazing fire to help you develop an organization that not only achieves the success you desire but also makes a positive contribution to society. Once the right culture permeates your organization, it becomes rock solid, and you will attract like-minded individuals who will carry the torch forward. With such commitment and passion, your organization can stand head and shoulders above others in your field.

# Acknowledgments

First and foremost, thank you to the dedicated Ideal Outcomes team who bravely signed up for our journey. May we continue to grow, thrive, and provide the SPARK to all our clients. None of this would be possible without your hard work and passion for excellence. I also must thank our clients who have partnered with us along the way.

This book would also not have been possible without the many extraordinary leaders who generously agreed to be interviewed for this book. Their encouragement and insights were invaluable.

Chris Augustine, Nielsen; Ann Hopkins Avery, Baker McKenzie; Chris Baggaley, Auto Club of Southern California; Andrea Belmont, Nielsen; Eileen Benwitt, Horizon Media; Justin Boyson, Chubb; Martin Bullis, Whole Foods Markets; Dan Calista, Vynamic; Richard Campo, Camden Property Trust; Steve Chikerotis, UniFirst Corporation; Tom Collingsworth, New Penn; Matteo Del Vecchio, Deconic; Jonathan Evans, ThyssenKrupp North America; Kerrian Fournier; Craig Gentry, formerly with Unilever Food Solutions; Steve Gonzalez, KONE Corporation; Jana Greenberg, Horizon Media; Stephen Hart, Federal Reserve Bank of Philadelphia; Matt Hawksley, BDP International; John Hren; Gary Kaplan, XL Catlin; David Katz, Randa Accessories; Andrew Koehler, ADP; Diane Leeming, AMITA Health; Charles Lilly, Hub International; Marcia Lyssy, BDP International; Tony Norris, Rosemount Flame and Gas/Emerson Automation Solutions; Hector Pena, Tailored Brands; Wil Reynolds, Seer Interactive; Shaun Rudy; Bala Sathyanarayanan, Xerox; Jennifer Speciale, McKinsey & Company; David Starr, Northern Trust Corporation; Paul Stout; Alan Tecktiel, Baker McKenzie; Emmet Vaughn, Exelon; Jason Watt, Cardinal Health; Tobias Witte, WITTBIX; Florence Zheng, Bentley Systems.

Finally, thank you to my editor Melanie Mulhall of Dragonheart for her insight and creativity, and gratitude to Malcolm Nicholl and Jeanne Kerr for their guidance and steadfast suggestions.

# Endnotes

**Introduction**

1. Heather R. Huhman, "Micromanagement Is Murder: So Stop Killing Your Employees," Entrepreneur.com, December 19, 2016, https://www.entrepreneur.com/article/286333.

2. Jim Harter and Annamarie Mann, "The Right Culture: Not Just About Employee Satisfaction," Gallup, April 12, 2017, https://news.gallup.com/businessjournal/208487/right-culture-not-employee-happiness.aspx.

**1 – The Key Is the Culture**

3. Thomas Kell and Gregory T. Carrott, "Culture Matters Most," *Harvard Business Review*, May 2005, https://hbr.org/2005/05/culture-matters-most.

4. Brooks Barnes, "Planned Sale of the Weinstein Company Collapses Again," *New York Times*, March 6, 2018, https://www.nytimes.com/2018/03/06/business/media/weinstein-company-sale.html.

**2 – The Impact of Culture**

5. Dan Pontefract, "If Culture Comes First, Performance Will Follow," *Forbes*, May 25, 2017, https://www.forbes.com/sites/danpontefract/2017/05/25/if-culture-comes-first-performance-will-follow/#5f7589896e62.

6. Shelley Pleiter, "Engaging Employees: Queen's partnership with Aon Hewitt celebrates 10 years of helping small- and medium-sized companies succeed," *Smith magazine*, Winter 2014, https://smith.queensu.ca/magazine/winter-2014/features/engaging-employees.

7. Dr. James Heskett and Dr. John Kotter, "Does corporate culture drive financial performance?" *Forbes*, February 10, 2011, https://www.forbes.com/sites/johnkotter/2011/02/10/does-corporate-culture-drive-financial-performance/#41b1034c7e9e.

8. "The Employee Experience Index: A new global measure of a human workplace and its impact," accessed May 4, 2018, http://www.globoforce.com/wpcontent/uploads/2016/10/The_Employee_Experience_Index.pdf.

9. "World's Leading Companies Failing Authenticity Test," FleishmanHillard, September 12, 2017, http://fleishmanhillard.com/2017/09/news-and-opinions/worlds-leading-companies-failing-authenticity-test/.

10. Geoff Beattie, "The Number One Thing Consumers Want From Brands? Honesty," Fast Company, November 14, 2014, https://www.fastcompany.com/3038488/the-number-one-thing-consumers-want-from-brands-honesty.

11. Beattie, "The Number One Thing…".

12. Christine Porath, "Half of Employees Don't Feel Respected by Their Bosses," *Harvard Business Review*, November 19, 2014, https://hbr.org/2014/11/half-of-employees-dont-feel-respected-by-their-bosses.

13. "Four Ways to Build a Talent Magnet Organization: Discover the keys to building a magnetic culture," Oracle, accessed July 17, 2018, https://go.oracle.com/hcm-four-ways-to-build-a-talent-magnet-organization.

14. https://www.traderjoes.com/.

15. https://www.glassdoor.com/Reviews/Trader-Joe-s-Reviews-E5631.htm.

16. Mark Mallinger and Gerry Rossy, "The Trader Joe's Experience: The impact of corporate culture on business strategy,"

*Graziado Business Review*, 2007, Volume 10, Issue 2, https://gbr.pepperdine.edu/2010/08/the-trader-joes-experience/.

17. Dave Hanna, "How to build a culture that withstands economic downturns," Inside HR, June 10, 2016, https://www.insidehr.com.au/how-to-build-a-culture-that-withstands-economic-downturns/.

18. "Global Leadership Forecast 2018," https://www.conference-board.org/globalleadershipforecast/.

### 3 – Getting from Here to There

19. https://www.unilever.com/about/who-we-are/our-history/.

### 4 – Defining Your Culture Through Purpose and Values

20. "Employee Engagement Drives Customer Satisfaction," TalentMap, accessed November 14, 2018, https://www.talentmap.com/employee-engagement-drives-customer-satisfaction/.

### 6 – Planning: Strategy and Process Alignment

21. "Report: Employee Engagement Benchmark Study, 2016," Temkin Group, February 16, 2016, https://experiencematters.blog/2016/02/16/report-employee-engagement-benchmark-study-2016/.

### 7 – Planning: People Make It Happen

22. "Four Ways to Build a Talent Magnet Organization: What It Takes to Attract and Retain Great People in Increasingly Competitive Talent Markets," Oracle, accessed November 14, 2018, http://www.oracle.com/us/products/applications/talent-magnet-3236631.pdf.

23. Dr. John Sullivan, "Bad Recruiting? It Can Cost Your Company a Whole Lot of Money," October 1, 2015, https://www.tlnt.com/bad-recruiting-it-can-cost-your-company-a-whole-lot-of-money/.

**8 – People Make It Happen**

24. James K. Harter, Frank L. Schmidt, Sangeeta Agrawal, and Stephanie K. Plowman, "The Relationship Between Engagement at Work and Organizational Outcomes: 2012 Q12® Meta-Analysis," Gallup, February 2013, https://employeeengagement.com/ wp-content/uploads/2013/04/2012-Q12-Meta-Analysis-Research-Paper.pdf.

25. Adam Bryant, "On a Scale of 1 to 10, How Weird Are You?" *New York Times*, January 9, 2010, https://www.nytimes.com/ 2010/01/10/business/10corner.html.

26. Dr. Al Lee, "25% Regret New Jobs: What to Consider When Considering a Job Offer," Payscale, November 30, 2007, https://www.payscale.com/career-news/2007/11/25-regret-new-j.

27. Blake Morgan, "Chief Culture Officer And Chief Customer Officer: A Winning Combination," *Forbes*, January 16, 2018, https://www.forbes.com/sites/blakemorgan/2018/01/16/chief-culture-officer-and-chief-customer-officer-a-winning-combination/#61db32cc3ab1.

28. Evelyn Orr, "Best Practice Series: Executive onboarding," Korn Ferry, January 14, 2015, https://www.kornferry.com/institute/best-practice-series-executive-onboarding.

29. Kevin Empey, "Ireland Performance Management Survey 2015: Performance Management is changing … but traditional approaches still dominate," Willis Towers Watson, March 2016, https://www.towerswatson.com/en/Insights/IC-Types/Survey-Research-Results/2016/03/Ireland-Performance-Management-Survey-2015.

30. Jenna Filipkowski, "Building a Coaching Culture with Managers and Leaders," Human Capital Institute, September 21, 2016, http://www.hci.org/hr-research/building-coaching-culture-managers-and-leaders.

31. "UniFirst Wins 2018 Stevie Award for Customer Service," March, 2018, https://unifirst.com/company/press-releases/unifirst-wins-2018-stevie-award-customer-service/.

## 9 – Sustaining the Change

32. Nitin Nohria and Michael Beer, "Cracking the Code of Change," *Harvard Business Review*, May-June, 2000, https://hbr.org/2000/05/cracking-the-code-of-change.

33. "Only One-Quarter of Employers Are Sustaining Gains From Change Management Initiatives, Towers Watson Survey Finds: Focus on manager's role could spark improvement in companies' ability to manage change," Willis Towers Watson, August 29, 2013, https://www.towerswatson.com/en/Press/2013/08/Only-One-Quarter-of-Employers-Are-Sustaining-Gains-From-Change-Management.

34. Amber Hurdle, *The Bombshell Business Woman: How to Become a Bold, Brave Female Entrepreneur* (Franklin, TN: Clovercroft Publishing, 2017).

35. Shelley DuBois, "The rise of the chief culture officer," *Fortune*, July 30, 2012, http://fortune.com/2012/07/30/the-rise-of-the-chief-culture-officer/.

36. "Tiny Pulse, The Era of Personal and Peer Accountability, 2015 Employee Engagement and Organizational Culture Report," https://cdn2.hubspot.net/hubfs/443262/pdf/2015_Employee_Engagement__Organizational_Culture_Report.pdf.

## 10 – Diversity and Millennials

37. Satya Nadella, *Hit Refresh: The Quest to Rediscover Microsoft's Soul and Imagine a Better Future for Everyone* (New York: Harper Business, 2017).

38. Thomas Barta, Markus Kleiner, and Tilo Neumann, "Is there a payoff from top-team diversity?" McKinsey Quarterly, April 2012,

https://www.mckinsey.com/business-functions/organization/our-insights/is-there-a-payoff-from-top-team-diversity.

39. Valentina Zarya, "The 2017 Fortune 500 Includes a Record Number of Women CEOs," June 7, 2017, http://fortune.com/2017/06/07/fortune-women-ceos/.

40. "Here Are The Largest Companies in America With Zero Black People on Their Boards," September 8, 2017, https://www.blackenterprise.com/companies-without-black-directors/.

41. Thomas Barta, Markus Kleiner, and Tilo Neumann, "Is there a payoff from top-team diversity?" McKinsey Quarterly, April 2012, https://www.mckinsey.com/business-functions/organization/our-insights/is-there-a-payoff-from-top-team-diversity.

42. "Diversity and Inclusion," https://careers.adidas-group.com/life-here/diversity?locale=en.

43. "Making Intel More Diverse," *Harvard Business Review*, March 10, 2017, https://hbr.org/ideacast/2017/03/making-intel-more-diverse.html.

44. "Making Intel More Diverse."

45. Larry Alton, "How Millennials Are Reshaping What's Important In Corporate Culture," *Forbes*, June 20, 2017, https://www.forbes.com/sites/larryalton/2017/06/20/how-millennials-are-reshaping-whats-important-in-corporate-culture/#3818a4402dfb.

46. Eddie Lou, "Why Millennials Want More Than Just Work: The Importance Of Your 'Double Bottom Line,'" *Forbes*, June 9, 2017, https://www.forbes.com/sites/theyec/2017/06/09/why-millennials-want-more-than-just-work-the-importance-of-your-double-bottom-line/#7b515c965784.

47. "Better Quality Of Work Life Is Worth A $7,600 Pay Cut For Millennials," Fidelity, April 7, 2016,

https://www.fidelity.com/about-fidelity/individual-investing/
better-quality-of-work-life-is-worth-pay-cut-for-millennials.

48. Jessica Brack & Kip Kelly, "Maximizing Millennials in the
Workplace," Kenan-Flagler, https://www.kenan-flagler.unc.edu/
executive-development/custom-
programs/%7E/media/DF1C11C056874DDA8097271A1ED48662.
ashx.

49. Amy Adkins, "Millennials: The Job-Hopping Generation,"
Gallup, May 12, 2016,
http://news.gallup.com/businessjournal/191459/millennials-
ob-hopping-generation.aspx.

50. Adkins, "Millennials: The Job-Hopping Generation."

51. Amy Adkins and Brandon Rigoni, "Managers: Millennials
Want Feedback, but Won't Ask for It," Gallup, June 2, 2016,
http://news.gallup.com/businessjournal/192038/managers-
millennials-feedback-won-ask.aspx.

52. "Millennials in Adulthood: Detached from Institutions,
Networked with Friends," Pew Research Center, March 7, 2014,
http://www.pewsocialtrends.org/2014/03/07/millennials-in-
adulthood/.

**11 – Global Considerations, Mergers, and Technology**

53. Vector Group Inc. http://vectorgroupinc.com/the-vector-
view-mergers-acquisitions-roadmap-for-success.

54. "Organizing for M&A: McKinsey Global Survey results,"
McKinsey & Company, December, 2011,
https://www.mckinsey.com/business-functions/strategy-and-
corporate-finance/our-insights/organizing-for-m-and-a-mckinsey-
global-survey-results.

55. Darcy Jacobsen, "6 Big Mergers That Were Killed by Culture
(And How to Stop it from Killing Yours)," Globoforce, September

26, 2012, https://resources.globoforce.com/globoforce-blog/6-big-mergers-that-were-killed-by-culture-and-how-to-stop-it-from-killing-yours.

56. Jenna Schnuer, "How to Blend Company Cultures in a Merger," *Entrepreneur*, March 22, 2011, https://www.entrepreneur.com/article/219333.

57. Ashley Goldsmith and Leighanne Levensaler, "Build a Great Company Culture with Help from Technology," *Harvard Business Review*, February 24, 2016, https://hbr.org/2016/02/build-a-great-company-culture-with-help-from-technology.

58. Steven Widen, "How Technology Impacts Work Culture," *Forbes*, October 5, 2017, https://www.forbes.com/sites/forbesagencycouncil/2017/10/05/how-technology-impacts-work-culture/#49986f1f721a.

59. Jeff Schwartz, Ardie van Berkel, Tom Hodson, and Ian Winstrom Otten, "The overwhelmed employee: Simplify the work environment," Deloitte Insights, March 7, 2014, https://www2.deloitte.com/insights/us/en/focus/human-capital-trends/2014/hc-trends-2014-overwhelmed-employee.html.

**12 – A Call to Action**

60. Larry Fink, "A Sense of Purpose: Annual Letter to CEOs," 2018, https://www.blackrock.com/corporate/investor-relations/larry-fink-ceo-letter.

61. "The Talent Forecast," Korn Ferry Institute, http://static.kornferry.com/media/sidebar_downloads/TalentForecastPart1.pdf.

62. "Profit vs Purpose: The Duel Begins," Korn Ferry Institute, May 15, 2018, https://www.kornferry.com/institute/the-duel-begins.

# About the Author

Jason Richmond is the President/CEO and Chief Culture Officer of Ideal Outcomes, Inc. During his career of more than twenty years, he has had the good fortune of working with companies of all sizes in a wide variety of industries. Jason has partnered with numerous start-up companies to help build solid foundations that have enabled them to become noted industry leaders. He has also worked closely with established Fortune 100 companies to create Leadership Development Journeys. In addition, Jason has provided thought leadership and innovative consulting services to a wide range of mid-size companies.

Over the course of his career, Jason has observed and captured best practices from successful organizations and integrated them into the core principles that form the foundation of Ideal Outcomes.

Jason's primary career focus began when he took the Dale Carnegie course after living and working in Australia for three years. He fully embraced Carnegie methods and philosophies as he witnessed how they impacted careers and companies around the world in such a positive way. This inspired Jason to partner with Dale Carnegie, which led to him becoming a valued resource for many organizations. In this capacity, he acted as an organizational development partner, helping companies implement talent development paths, culture maps, succession plans, and learning strategies.

This stimulating career path provided Jason the opportunity to travel the world and collaborate with a talented collection of professionals in a multitude of international cultures.

Through Ideal Outcomes, Jason shares what he's discovered. His mission is to draw from his experiences and apply the lessons he's learned to his life, his team members' lives, and his clients' business challenges.

Jason believes that you don't learn if you remain stationary. This is why he continues to dedicate his life and career to continuous improvement. Ultimately, Ideal Outcomes does everything it can to make the lives of its clients better, which in turn benefits the organizations they serve. Jason achieves this by connecting closely with each of his clients on an authentic human level while working to foster energetic business cultures that exude the characteristics that define the people they most trust and admire.